Analogia Entis

Analogia Entis

On the Analogy of Being, Metaphysics, and the Act of Faith

STEVEN A. LONG

University of Notre Dame Press

Notre Dame, Indiana

University of Notre Dame Press
Notre Dame, Indiana 46556
www.undpress.nd.edu
All Rights Reserved

Copyright © 2011 by University of Notre Dame

Published in the United States of America

Library of Congress Cataloging-in-Publication Data

Long, Steven A.
   Analogia entis : on the analogy of being, metaphysics, and the act of faith / by Steven A. Long.
       p. cm.
   Includes bibliographical references (p.   ) and index.
   ISBN-13: 978-0-268-03412-2 (pbk. : alk. paper)
   ISBN-10: 0-268-03412-5 (pbk. : alk. paper)
  1. Thomas, Aquinas, Saint, 1225?–1274. 2. Analogy. 3. Metaphysics.
 4. Analogy (Religion) I. Title.
   B765.T54L63 2011
   111—dc23
                                                                2011025680

Contents

Acknowledgments

I should particularly like to thank John F. Boyle from the University of St. Thomas for the benefit of his comments and criticisms, for his unfailing jeweler's eye with respect to speculative inquiry, and most of all for his friendship: who could ask for a more condignly Thomistic inspiration than this? The present work also is indebted to Reinhard Huetter of Duke University, for whose judicious encouragement and insight I am grateful. Likewise, am I indebted to a man with whom I disagree, in the course of the very manuscript below, regarding the nature of analogy: our late and beloved Ralph McInerny. He encouraged me to pursue this manuscript and its publication, having seen an early version, and while clearly differing with me regarding the question, strongly sympathized with my criticisms of the overemphasis on causal relation and participation as tantamount to the analogy of being. His extraordinary gift for encouraging serious engagement, and his exemplary joy and wisdom, will be missed wherever minds gather to pursue the *scientia* sought and developed by Aquinas (no one was ever less snookered by the attempted reduction of speculative life to historicist text-juggling and word searches than he). Of course, I would be lacking were I not also to mention here the friendship and counsel of Fr. Romanus Cessario, OP, whose appreciation of this work has been the strongest of encouragements; as likewise, Russell Hittinger, who—although remote by dint of simple necessity from the composition of this work—as teacher and friend inspires my efforts. Here I would also like to thank the late Fr. Jan Walgrave, OP, my old mentor from Louvain, with whom during my stay in Belgium I had the grace of weekly conversations of a strictly speculative nature. I should very much like to know what he would make of the ensuing analysis, which our conversations about analogy have in part engendered. But far beyond this, I mention him here because I am grateful for his pronounced encouragement to engage not in secondhand philosophy and theology, but in theology and philosophy proper; and because of the luminosity of his person and his witness as a profound and contemplative Dominican theologian and philosopher.

I owe heartfelt thanks to my generous colleagues from Ave Maria University, whose intellectual and spiritual engagement and example are a constant invitation and stimulus to reflection, research, and richer converse with the Catholic intellectual tradition. I am grateful in particular to Michael Waldstein, Gregory Vall, and Joseph Trabbic for their intelligent appreciation and encouragement of my work.

Last, I mention what is also in principle first: the understanding of my family, which at times is of course for them more like the cloud of unknowing (what Dad is doing in the study is important: but *what* is he doing in there and *how much longer* will it take?). Writing imposes sacrifices on both authors and their families. Because this work seeks to contribute to the absolutely necessary recrudesence of metaphysics within theological contemplation, and so to serve the wider needs of the Church, one hopes that it—at least in intention, if not in execution—is worthy of the sacrifices that enabled it to be composed. I am grateful to my wife, Anna

Maria Long, and to our seven children, who not only enabled this to be written through their sacrifices, but who manifest for me anew, each day, the inscape of the *analogia entis*, the likeness of diverse *rationes* of act, as manifest in their diverse characters, gifts, individual predilections, strengths, and weaknesses—for being is not only generically and specifically, but also individually, diversified and analogous. Perhaps a Catholic husband and father is optimally situated to see that the actual being of creatures is prior to their necessary relatedness to God and others, even though the latter is *pari passu* with the former. Family life teaches the humility, the joy, the suffering, and the ecstasis of being in a unique manner. We do not push this ladder aside after climbing it, as our individually diverse being endures even in beatific vision; and as St. Teresa of Avila reminds us, no matter how sublimely our contemplation may rise, it never transcends the humanity of Christ.

Introduction

The following work has been inspired by the conviction that a generation and more of historically nuanced and profound contemplation of the metaphysics and theology of Thomas Aquinas nonetheless has managed, in the density of the historical foliage, to mislay central doctrinal tenets of the Angelic Doctor. Moreover, these tenets are precisely those that prove most essential to the metaphysician and the theologian: in particular, those that concern the intrinsic analogicity of being as divided by act and potency, an analogical division that is the foundation both for the doctrine of participation and for the causal demonstrations proving the truth of the proposition that God exists. Instead, whether in process theology, in the Catholic theologians of the *Communio* school, or in Thomists such as Montagnes, one finds free-floating relation taken as the metaphysical basis for the analogy of being and hence for theism. This is a systematically untenable situation, and it is in significant part to remedy it that this work is written.

Of course, this work concurs with the writings of certain older Thomists—e.g., Maritain, Anderson, Garrigou-Lagrange—unjustly impugned as somehow historically insensitive because they refused to submerge speculative questions in historical obscuration. There is little point in putting the matter more gently: as we shall see below, it has come to be assumed that because he does not expressly revisit it in later works, Thomas abandoned his teaching on analogy from *De veritate*. By the conclusion of this work, I hope the reader may see why this position struck earlier generations of Thomists—and strikes this author—as rather like saying that Thomas changed his views on noncontradiction as the first principle because he did not substantially re-engage it in the *tertia pars* of the *Summa theologiae*. To my mind, the systematic consideration of this question has not properly been pursued. I will argue that the systematic reasons for the affirmation of the analogy of being as the analogy of proper proportionality persist unabated from *De veritate* forward—indeed, that they grow stronger—and are actually stated in the *Summa theologiae* even though they are not brought forward to address this precise question. (Indeed, one might think, Thomas already explicitly answered it in *De veritate* and so had no need to raise it again, especially since there is no contradiction between the two treatments.)

My account of the relation between *De veritate* and the *Summa theologiae* will be found later in this work. Not the least confusion that has long bewildered people is Thomas's seeming emphasis upon analogy of attribution and proportion in the *Summa theologiae*, while earlier, in *De veritate*, he argued for proper proportionality as the analogy of being and as alone capable of avoiding the error of affirming God to have a determined relation to creatures.

Analogy of proper proportionality implies no determined relation of the analogates: e.g., "as light is to the eye, so is truth to the mind" does not render light to be truth, or the eye to be the mind. Rather, a similarity of diverse *rationes* of act is discerned, which one may call "illumination"—but this "illumination" is not tantamount merely to one thing, one univocal object, but is analogous, applying to the two cases proportionately. Such analogy is the way in which we grasp the division of being by act and potency, in terms of the likeness of diverse *rationes* of act: e.g., as the frog is to its act of being, so the angel is to its act of being; or, as potentially walking is to actually walking, so potentially whistling is to actually whistling.

Standing in contrast to analogy of proper proportionality as the analogy of being are the analogy of attribution and analogy of proportion. Analogy of attribution extends the meaning of a term from its central proper case—for instance, health as centrally pertaining to a living organism—to causes, effects, or signs that are not properly and intrinsically designated by the term. Hence medicine is said to be healthy as a cause of the health of the organism, but is not itself a proper subject of health. Simple analogy of proportion implies determined relations: e.g., the proportion of nickel to dime implies the determined relation of five to ten, because the distance from the nickel to the dime is the same as the distance from the dime to the nickel. By contrast, while the creature has a real determined relation to God, God has no real determined relation to the creature, because God infinitely—that is, by no mere finite increment—transcends the creature. Thus although Thomas allowed in *De veritate* that one might speak of an analogy of what he called transferred proportion as long as the comparison of any one to any other "boils down to" or is retranslatable in terms of proper proportionality, there neither is nor can be any strict analogy of proportion between creature and God. As will be shown below, Thomas's example of transferred proportion in *De veritate*, q. 23, art. 7, ad 9, is "sicut se habet princeps ad civitatem ita gubernator ad navim," or "as the ruler is to the city, so is the pilot to his ship"—a classic illustration of proper proportionality. His later insistence on analogy of proportion between creature and God is consistent with this emphasis in *De veritate*.

Likewise, with respect to analogy of attribution of created effect to divine cause: while the effect is always attributed to the cause, and so analogy of creature to God will always be treated by Thomas attributively, the being of the creature is not God. Rather, being is predicated of the creature itself: and it is on the basis of the being of creatures that the truth of the proposition that God exists is demonstrated. As nonexistent beings are not attributable as real effects, the analogy of being is prior to the analogy of attribution and is in fact its necessary condition. While the analogy of being does not substitute for causal analysis, the analogy of being as the likeness of diverse *rationes* of act is the foundation and precondition for causal resolution to God. Further, while the effect is attributed to God, God is not attributed to the effect, i.e., God is not essentially "cause of Steven Long." Inasmuch as God infinitely transcends the created effect, there is no determined relation of God to created effect, which means that the attributive analogy of creature to God presupposes and must be "backwards translatable" into the analogy of proper proportionality that as the creature is to what is its own, so God is to what is His own.

Relation to God—the relation of createdness, the causal relation of participation—presupposes the being of the creature inasmuch as nonexistent beings have no real relations (and God is not really related to the creature). Hence the analogy of being is necessarily ontologically prior to participation and the relation to God. Attributive analogies of created effect to God as first cause, and of proportion of one to another, always presuppose, and must be finally retranslated into, the analogy of being as an analogy of proper proportionality regarding the likeness of diverse *rationes* of act as limited by potency. Seeing this, however, requires speculative understanding of Thomas's teaching in *De veritate*; it also suggests the value of understanding that the formal reign of a principle in a science is not necessarily best determined by counting words.

The internecine controversies within Thomism over the nature of the analogy of being are famous, as likewise are the misplaced allegations of "onto-theology" and reductionism which—condign as they are for most post-Enlightenment thought—have no point of genuine contact with the teaching of Aquinas.[1] The controversy regarding analogy of being taken up within this work, however, is singularly disruptive inasmuch as it clouds the essential conditions for all knowledge of God and for the understanding of the transcendence and intelligibility of the act of faith.

One senses that for some theologians it might be a happy event to be able to treat our knowledge of God, or of the theological character of the act of faith, without any reference to metaphysics. Alas, this is impossible, not only because revelation is given to us in human language and so carries with it human categories, but also because revelation pertains both to God Who is the creator of all finite being and to creation in relation to God: it presupposes *natura*. Hence, the relation of the being of things to God, and the truth that God is first cause of the being of creatures, are doubly written into revelation itself, both as primordial revelation in creation and as supernatural revelation strictly speaking. Accordingly, there are only two possibilities: that the being common to finite things (or as Thomas agreeing with Aristotle would say, the being said of substance and the categories) is intelligible in such a way as to render possible a contemplation of God that does not reduce or deny the transcendence of God; or else created being is such that no intelligible speech of God is possible proceeding from finite being.

Someone might ask whether there is not a third possibility. Could there not be speech about God that God Himself authorizes and that so escapes any taint of created categories? To which the response is that even human speech inspired by God remains both human and speech; and that if such speech were to be wholly denuded of any created intelligibility, it would by that fact be wholly unintelligible to the human creature and thereby cease to be speech since speech is more than sound whose signification is either unknowable or nonexistent. It would follow that all theology would become some species of advanced glossolalia, and that seeking to derive any rational implications from it would be impossible. Further, there would of course literally be no language in which it could so much as be suggested why Christian belief should be received as meaningful, much less as true. For the very idea of transcendence is—dare one say it?—an idea, that is, it posits that God has no real relation of dependence on creatures, but rather that creatures depend wholly upon God. Hence, if analogy of being does not pertain to all ideas and judgments of the real from the start, there will be no possibility of speaking of God without placing God in a determined relation to the perfection of the creature and so reducing the transcendence of God. This is to say that we are returned to the original position: either being is analogous and so affords the possibility of intelligible discourse regarding God, or being is not analogous and so there is no such possibility of intelligible discourse about God.

In framing the issue in this way, one means no discourtesy to Scotus, whose preoccupation was to assure precisely that our reasoning regarding God would be safeguarded. Yet he labored under the erroneous judgment that only univocal concepts and judgments could assure that the middle term in our reasoning would not be equivocal. And it is indeed the much contemned Cajetan who corrects this error in accord with the doctrine of Aquinas. But to understand his correction requires something rather more even than a deep appreciation of its virtues as a semantic theory,[2] for the metaphysical doctrine of Aristotle, and further of Aquinas, is greatly implicated here.

Accordingly, as there is indeed no way around the metaphysical flame, this work undertakes to show how it is that Arisotle and later Thomas are able to pass through it without being consumed in the fire of univocality or denial of divine transcendence. This is, by the way, an occasion to correct certain erroneous readings of Aristotle that deny he should be credited with upholding the divine transcendence. Though he lacked the ability to show what Thomas made clear—namely, how divine providence did not imply God being determined by creatures—Aristotle upheld absolute divine transcendence to the point that he preferred to deny divine knowledge of creatures rather than compromise the divine transcendence in the least degree. It is truly past time for this doctrinal and historical fact to replace the proposition urged by some that pagan thought could not rise to God save as the "highest part of the world." For this proposition is simply false of the thought of Aristotle inasmuch as it requires that God be subject to a reciprocal causality from creatures which Aristotle does not admit. Where does Aristotle allow that God depends upon anything outside of the divine nature, or that anything can effect alteration in God? For God to be merely "part of a whole" or the highest part of the world, God must be dependent upon the world to be. This is not the case with Aristotle, for whom God is not merely "the highest part of the world" but utterly transcendent of the world, in absolutely no dependence on the world. It is one thing for philosophers to apply a method; it is another for them to deny historico-doctrinal data where these do not accommodate their method. I refer, of course, to the important work of Fr. Sokolowski, *The God of Faith and Reason*, an instructive and genuinely profound work,[3] which yet insofar as it suggests that creation is a doctrine knowable only through revelation, implies negation both of the teaching of Aquinas, for whom it is naturally demonstrable,[4] and of Aquinas's clear judgment that this doctrine of creation is to be found in the teaching of Aristotle.[5]

It is of course common today to begin either with more general logical or semantic concerns or with extensive textual considerations, but we begin here with a purely speculative problem whose analysis is shared by Aristotle and Aquinas and which is essential to metaphysical *scientia*: the problem of Parmenidean monism. This is a problem that stands athwart the very entryway to metaphysics. Without adequate speculative penetration of this foundational consideration, the approach to the analogy of being is vitiated.

Accordingly, the order of this work is as follows: First, it addresses the aforesaid Parmenidean problem and its solution, representing the strong element of continuity that binds the thought of Aristotle and Thomas. I will consider this problem summarily rather than in a full historico-doctrinal presentation because the purpose for its consideration is purely speculative. It is in relation to this problem that the fundamental analogicity of being that is our speculative object becomes clear. Second, following upon this consideration of the metaphysical foundations, we will give in brief exegetic/doctrinal metaphysical arguments for viewing the analogy of being as that of the likeness of diverse *rationes* of act and potency (a doctrine perfected rather than transmuted by Aquinas in his full articulation of the real distinction of essence and existence).[6] Third, I will reply to the most prominent objections both to the understanding of the *analogia entis* as an analogy of proper proportionality founded upon the division of being by act and potency, and to the view that Thomas persisted in holding this teaching.[7] Only after engaging these prominent objections will I, fourth, briefly address the import of the analogy of being as not only the foundation of all knowledge of God, but also as a safeguard to the intelligibility and transcendence of the act of faith, and as a manifestation of the persistent integral importance of metaphysics within theological method. Fifth, and finally, I offer an appendix addressing the vexed question of the nature of the analogical "abstraction" to be found in the negative existential judgment of *separatio* which lies at the root of the discovery of being as subject matter for a science: what Thomas refers to in the *Summa theologiae* as "abstraction through composition and division" (*ST*, I, q. 85, art. 1, ad 1).

The importance of all this is more than a simple corrective reallocation of scholarly attention from one part of Thomas's corpus to another, or yet another *sed contra* to Barthian fideism. The point is to draw attention to the unity and coherence of Thomas's metaphysics and its centrality both in instructing us on the foundation of our knowledge of God and in safeguarding the intelligibility and transcendence of the act of faith.

This book is thus, in a sense, a primer addressing the most decisive metaphysical issue for theologians. But it is no introductory work, because it presupposes familiarity with the terms introduced in this prologue, and thus implicitly with the metaphysics of *esse* and with the context of modern and postmodern negations of the *praeambula fidei* and of the essential role of metaphysics within theological method. Metaphysics within theological method is subordinated to the formal object of the theologian: God and all things as related to God, whether known through supernatural revelation or proportionate natural truth.

Lest I be guilty of impiety, let me pay tribute here to two authors in particular: Jacques Maritain, whose metaphysical acumen is arresting, and James Francis Anderson. The references to Maritain in this work should speak for themselves of this author's high regard for his thoughts on the foundation of metaphysics. As for Anderson, after completing this work, I reread John Knasas's fine work *Being and Some Twentieth Century Thomists*. In the notes, I saw his reference to Anderson's book *The Bond of Being*[8] and his mention of a text indicating that Anderson saw that the analogy of being is prior to the relation to God. Knasas did not, to my mind, understand this so well as he did the many other complex issues he sorts through in his book. As he puts it:

> James Anderson, *The Bond of Being*, lucidly argues for analogy of proportionality as the analogy between God and creatures. In Thomistic texts that speak of analogy of proportion between God and creatures (Aquinas, *S.T.* I, 13, 5c, and *C.G.* I, 35) Anderson argues that we do not have a distinct type of analogy but a mix of proportionality and proportion. In the mix, proportionality is basic (*The Bond of Being*, 248–49). Formally speaking there is proportionality; materially, there is proportion (232–33). Anderson's position leads to this strange expression: "Once more, however, it must be pointed out that the very being itself of the creature does not consist in its *relation to* God: the relation itself is ontologically posterior to the being of the creature" (119). This remark seems to say that the *ontologically prior* situation is an independence of God and creatures.[9]

While Anderson speaks of formal proportionality and material proportion, I prefer the language of *De veritate* regarding "transferred proportion" as a proportion that necessarily must be expressible in terms of proper proportionality: but it is the same insight. Further, what Knasas calls the ontologically prior situation for the creature is on Anderson's (and my) account, not independence of God: if anything is "ontologically prior to creation" for the creature, it is not relation—God has no real relation to the creature—but nothingness. Nonexistent beings have no real relations. Hence only *pari passu* with God's bestowal of being to the creature—and only because of that being—is the creature really related to God. It may sound good to say that the creature is constituted by its relation to God, but this is not true: the creature is not constituted by its relation to God, but by God; and for God to constitute or cause is not for God to change or be really related, but for the creature to be. The effect of God is the very being of the creature; insofar and inasmuch as the creature exists, it is therefore related to God as its cause. God is not really related to the creature, and the creature is really related to God inasmuch as it exists, as it has being. Hence the analogical formality of being is prior to and the basis of the real relations of creatures to God, and it is necessarily ontologically prior to the relation of createdness, prior to the relation of causal participation (the creature participates nothing until it exists).

Anderson saw this crucial point, a point that has been forgotten in the intervening years, although he seems not to have articulated it as clearly and strategically, nor explained it as thoroughly, as I try to do below. He consigns it to a marginal comment; but at that time no one had yet made the argument that the analogy of being should be viewed as nothing other than the causal relation of participation. (*The Bond of Being* was published in 1949—even the work of Lyttkens is subsequent, to say nothing of Klubertanz, Montagnes, et alia.) In any case, having read some of his work years ago, I did not recollect his analysis until after writing the present book. I am as happy to have discovered the same truth, as likewise I am now to honor Anderson—an insufficiently appreciated author—for his insight: an insight that should not have fallen from view in the many ensuing constructions of the analogy of being as simply equivalent with the analogy of causal relation and participation.

It is a salient insistence of this present work that causal relation and participation are founded—both in reality and in our knowledge—upon being as analogically divided by act and potency. If nothing exists, nothing is causally related, and so the creature must with ontological priority be in order to be causally related; and it is only proceeding from our knowledge of beings according to their diverse *rationes* of act as limited by potency that we infer the reality of the first cause, or discriminate beings according to their hierarchic participation.

To sum up: in this work, I have tried to present as clearly as possible the fundamentality of the analogy of being in metaphysics, and its close relation to the first principle of noncontradiction and to the overcoming of Parmenidean monism. Likewise this work responds to various prominent Thomistic scholars who deny that the analogy of being is a likeness of diverse measures of act as limited in relation to potency. I have also tried to make clear how essential the analogy of being is for the transcendence and intelligibility of all reference to God and thus for the act of faith itself.

The present work seeks to address its subject—the analogy of being—with maximal metaphysical speculative formality and clarity. The very foundation of metaphysics, and the aid given by metaphysics to the theologian, are at stake. For this reason, bringing out the coherence, solidity, penetration, and unity of Thomas's metaphysics and the corresponding aid it brings theology, is my entire object. As subordinated to the theological object of contemplating God and all things in relation to God, metaphysics serves *sacra doctrina*. It does so especially by articulating the analogy of being upon which all causal inference to God, and all relatedness of creature to God, is founded, and which the superanalogy of faith necessarily presupposes.

First Principles and the Challenge
of Parmenidean Monism

It surely is beyond cavil that for both Aristotle and Thomas the principle of noncontradiction is radically first, for without it, no intelligible consideration is possible. But it is often not grasped that this principle is not primarily a logical, but rather—as Aristotle's consideration of it in the *Metaphysics* would suggest—a metaphysical one. Being, that which is, is a real principle. And the principle of noncontradiction articulates the truth that being is not nonbeing. One grants that nonbeing is purely conceptual—were it to exist, it would not be nonbeing. But being is not purely conceptual, and the truth articulated by the principle refers to being. Just as one may truly affirm that one's sister is not a genus—or that God is not a creature, something that would be true even were no creatures to exist since the divine nature is not and cannot be created—so it is a real rather than merely conceptual distinction to divide being from nonbeing. Although the principle of noncontradiction does not articulate a real plurality—nor a real relation, since non-existent beings do not have real relations—it does articulate a real distinction founded upon being: by the very ontologically positive character of being, it is not nonbeing, and this follows from the very nature of being. Thus, act is not non-act. Nietzsche of course famously objects that were the principle of noncontradiction true, man would need to enjoy some prior knowledge of being; but that since this is not true, the principle of noncontradiction is a mere imposition of the mind upon the real:

> We are unable to affirm and to deny one and the same thing: this is a subjective empirical law, not the expression of any "necessity" but only of an inability.
>
> If, according to Aristotle, the law of contradiction is the most certain of all principles, if it is the ultimate and most basic, upon which every demonstrative proof rests, if the principle of every axiom lies in it; then one should consider all the more rigorously what presuppositions already lie at the bottom of it. *Either it asserts something about actuality, about being, as if one already knew this from another source*; that is, as if opposite attributes could not be ascribed to it. Or the proposition means: opposite attributes should not be ascribed to it. In that case, logic would be an imperative, not to know the true, but to posit and arrange a world that shall be called true by us.
>
> In short, the question remains open: are the axioms of logic adequate to reality or are they a means and measure for us to create reality, the concept "reality," for ourselves?—*To affirm the former one would, as already said, have to have a previous knowledge of being—which is certainly not the case.* The proposition therefore contains no criterion of truth, but an imperative concerning that which should count as true. [Emphasis mine.][1]

But, to the contrary, every negation presupposes a prior affirmation. It is true enough that for the negation of negation to imply something ontologically positive, a real subject is required. But in affirming that being is not nonbeing, the principle of noncontradiction begins with a real subject, and denies that this subject is identical with its negation. Is this beginning with a real subject something simply "made up" by the mind and imposed on the real as a sort of Nietzschean imperative? No. The mind has *contactus* with the real from the very beginning, the sense eliciting the sensible, and the intellect eliciting the intelligible. Being is the first intelligible, as sound is the first audible (*ST*, I, q. 5, art. 2, resp.)—all knowledge occurs in terms of it. Even the identification of purely conceptual being is possible only because of the contradistinction with real being. Far from needing some leap of faith to have contact with the real, the human person is cognitively immersed in the real from the start beyond his feeble capacities fully to appreciate it.

The problem of Parmenides derives from the realization that outside of being there is nothing. Yet being is self-identical with itself, and so seemingly excludes otherness and multiplicity; it is immobile and so seemingly incompatible with change; there is nothing outside of being that could limit it, and so seemingly it is incompatible with limit. Change cannot proceed from being, first because being already is, and also because inasmuch as being is not nonbeing, it cannot "change" so as to be nonbeing. Nor can change proceed from nonbeing, because nonbeing is not. Hence change in every way appears impossible to reconcile with the principle of noncontradiction. Yet when we look out the window, we see many, limited, changing beings.

Neither Aristotle nor Aquinas thought that a response to Parmenides was needed to safeguard the realism of the intelligible perception that there is manyness, limit, and change in the world. Indeed, one can almost hear the audible sigh of the analytic practitioner for whom this whole consideration is simply a "false problem." Yet to know the evidence on the basis of which an account (in this case, that of Parmenides) is false, is not yet necessarily to know how to reconcile that evidence with the first principle of being and knowing, the principle of noncontradiction. Until this reconciliation occurs, it will seem either that one must follow Parmenides into a monism not so dissimilar to that of Nargarjuna and other Eastern mystics, or else deny that the principle of noncontradiction is a real principle. Yet neither of these options will serve.

Of course, Plato develops his doctrine of participation in large measure as a way of showing how things may be both like and unlike. He does so by articulating their participation in the forms of likeness and unlikeness, and by placing unity at the level of form rather than of sensible particular. Hypostatizing the form, however, runs athwart the intelligible perception that form is in things just as much as the Parmenidean monism runs athwart the perception of manyness, limit, and change. Moreover, there are indeed many forms, and even if these are viewed as somehow derivative from the Form of forms, it suggests manyness and limit within being even if change has somehow been held outside of being in the realm of the mere sensible "shadows of the forms." The cumulative Aristotelian criticism of the Platonic doctrine of form concerns the affirmation not merely of the intelligibility of change and motion, but also of the intelligibility of limit and multiplicity, both of which are essential to the very doctrine of the forms. Each form itself is distinct from other forms: but if being is self-identical and unlimited, on what basis can it be many, diverse, and limited? Hence, inasmuch as one grants that the doctrine of participation in the Forms is of itself incapable of reconciling our intelligible perceptions with the principle of noncontradiction, we are left again with the unacceptable alternative of monism, or, the denial of noncontradiction as a real principle.

In the course of responding to Parmenides regarding the first principle of noncontradiction—a metaphysical principle—Aristotle affirms that being is divided by potency and act. The Vatican Congregation for Studies would later place this as the very first of the twenty-four Thomistic theses, which were of course meant as invitations in the intelligible order and not as the purely praxic and disciplinary accretions for which they were soon to be taken and then forgotten. Aristotle argues that there is in being a principle that is not merely nonbeing, for it is a real capacity; not merely possibility, because it is always dependent upon a prior act to which it is related;[2] and not act, because it is precisely real subjective capacity or potency founded upon act and distinct from it. Prior to being sculpted, the clay is sculptable: but it is not yet actually to the least degree sculpted, it is merely potentially sculpted. Prior to moving, I am potentially in motion but actually at rest. Prior to considering an argument, I am potentially considering the argument, but actually, let us say, enjoying a piece of music. And so forth. Every potency presupposes the actual subject of the potency, yet as potency it is not in act. Hence, change does not proceed from the form of the thing changed—wood as such does not become ash, because wood is wood; but it proceeds from the matter of the wooden thing, enabling that thing to receive a different substantial form which is actually educed from the matter. Form, matter, and privation characterize change, and matter is clearly *potentia*. Hence while the account of potency and act is initially articulated in terms of the analysis of sensible being and change, and so enters into the ontology of nature or physics, nonetheless, inasmuch as it pertains to the reconciliation of the first principle of being with our experience of sensible being, it is also of actual and implicit metaphysical value from the start.

As Aristotle puts it in *Meta*. IX, 1, being is divided with respect to act and potency, a distinction that he articulates further in *Meta*. IX, 6, 1048a30–1048b9:

Actuality, then, is the existence of a thing not in the way which we express by "potentially"; we say that potentially, for instance, a statue of Hermes is in the block of wood and the half-line is in the whole, because it might be separated out, and we call even the man who is not studying a man of science, if he is capable of studying; the thing that stands in contrast to each of these exists actually. Our meaning can be seen in the particular cases by induction, and we must not seek a definition of everything but be content to grasp the analogy, that it is as that which is building is to that which is capable of building, and the waking to the sleeping, and that which is seeing to that which has its eyes shut but has sight, and that which has been shaped out of the matter to the matter, and that which has been wrought up to the unwrought. Let actuality be defined by one member of this antithesis, and the potential by the other. But all things are not said in the same sense to exist actually, but only by analogy—as A is in B or to B, C is in D or to D; for some are as movement to potency, and the others as substance to some sort of matter.[3]

In short, act and potency are knowable only inductively, and if one cannot so much as intelligently perceive these in all their analogical variety, there is a sense in which one cannot be helped. Of course, what is at stake is not the dumb, insensate Humean sense of induction, wherein sheer mulitiplicity of common perception beats an anticipation into our sensibility. No, this is an intelligent perception and insight into reality, that reality which contrary to Hume is indeed subject to necessity. (The principle of noncontradiction is not merely conceptual but real!) As the potency to laugh is to actually laughing, so is the potency to thought to actually thinking, or the potency to cook to actually cooking: yet laughing is not thinking, nor is thinking cooking. There is a likeness of diverse *rationes* of act and potency.[4] Of course, this extends beyond operation to substance: by reason of its potential principle of materiality, the thing that is wooden is potentially ash. Transmutative potencies are distinct from active potencies, yet they share a certain likeness of proportionality. As Aristotle puts it in *Meta.* XI, 9, 1065b15–16: "There being a distinction in each class of things between the potential and the completely real, I call the actuality of the potential as such, movement." Potency and act divide being. Indeed, in the *Eudemian Ethics*, Aristotle's clear metaphysical sense of motion as any transition from potency to act extends to the realm of the human spirit in a way strongly suggestive of the later teaching of Aquinas (and reminiscent even of the technical precisions with which this teaching is rendered by Domingo Bañez):

Yet someone may raise the question whether fortune is the cause of precisely this—forming a desire for the right thing at the right time. Or, on that showing, will not fortune be the cause of everything—even of thought and deliberation? since it is not the case, that one only deliberates when one has deliberated even previously to that deliberation, nor does one only think when one has previously thought before thinking, and so on to infinity, but there is some starting-point; therefore thought is not the starting-point of thinking, nor deliberation of deliberating. Then what else is, save fortune? It will follow that everything originates from fortune. Or shall we say that there is a certain starting-point outside which there is no other, and that this, merely owing to its being of such and such a nature, can produce a result of such and such a nature? But this is what we are investigating—what is the starting-point of motion in the spirit? The answer then is clear: as in the universe, so there, everything is moved by God; for in a manner the divine element in us is the cause of all our motions. And the starting-point of reason is not reason but something superior to reason. What, then, could be superior even to knowledge and to intellect, except God? (*Eud. Eth.* VII, 14, 1248a16–29)[5]

This, by the way, rather clearly indicates the efficiency of the divine causality, as it is a productive cause—a point mirrored even in the text that is often cited as proving that for Aristotle God moves only as a final but not as an efficient cause.[6]

It might be thought that we are not yet beyond the threshold of the physics, since the development of the understanding of potency is in terms of sensible being in its change, motion, limit, and mulitiplicity. Yet what this misses is that it pertains to being to be divided into potency and act. The principle of noncontradiction does not at some point become transmuted to *become* a metaphysical principle, for it is already one from the start. While the discovery of being as the subject matter of a science occurs late in the order of learning and discovery, being and its principles are present to us from the beginning, awaiting only our abstractive intuition—by way of judgment in the act of *separatio*, to be sure, and yet abstractive because not focusing precisely upon lesser formalities than that of being as such which nonetheless are inviscerate within being. The view that the response to Parmenides is exclusively physical loses sight of the datum that the being common to substance and the categories is being nonetheless, despite the datum that we initially know sensible being (or being as sensible) prior to knowing immaterial being. Indeed, there is in a real sense no such thing as *ens mobile*: there is only *ens in quantum mobile*, because to be mobile a thing must first be. Indeed, the argument for real distinction of essence and existence in *De ente et essentia* sets out from substance and the categories as understood relative to the proper object of the intellect, namely, quiddity in corporeal matter. Certainly quiddity in corporeal matter is not merely *ens mobile*, while of course *ens mobile* is truly known in reference to material quiddity. There is always implicitly not only a being subject to motion and change, but a "what" which defines the character of subject (in terms of essence), change, and motion (these last two in terms of the nature or whatness of the principle from and toward which the motion or change proceeds).

But does it not appear that prior to the actual demonstration of the spiritual soul or of God, material being might be equivalent to being *qua* being? No. The reason is comparatively simple and is given by Aristotle himself in the beginning of the *Metaphysics.*[7] Being is not a genus, whereas "material being" designates a genus or quasi-genus. But whereas the genus does not formally include its *differentiae* on pain of implying that all members of a genus must belong to a given species, being must include all its differences, because if it does not they will not be. Hence, from the start, and regarding substance and the categories, it is clear that these are and that being is irreducible to any genus.

It is true that in the *Summa contra gentiles*, I, 12, Thomas writes: "For, as it is said in the *Metaphysics* IV, if there is no knowable substance higher than sensible substance, there will be no science higher than physics." But note that the conditional pertains to "knowable substance" and not "actually known" substance, i.e., the proposition is not that one must actually know there is subsistent immaterial being in order to discover the subject matter of metaphysics; the proposition is that there must be a knowable substance higher than sensible substance for metaphysics to be a science, whether it is known at the outset or not being a different question. That is, for one who is aware of what metaphysical science is, and who develops it fully enough, it will be apparent that it could not be a science were there to be no substance higher than sensible substance; but it does not follow that the discovery of the subject matter of being *qua* being is impossible prior to this realization. Likewise, if there were to be no God, there could be no natural law, for natural law is merely a rational participation of the eternal law; but for Aquinas, our initial discovery of the natural law does not necessarily entail immediate realization that its intelligibility strongly implies and requires the reality of the eternal law.

But genus and species are logical categories, so is not the observation that being is not a genus a merely logical observation? Well, the original question—as to whether being might not be equivalent with material being—was evidently asking whether being is merely something logical: to which we have already seen that the answer is, no. And if we ask whether being comprises anything other than the sum total of the members of the quasi-genus of material being, the very condition for affirming of these diverse substances that they are is already the perception of the analogicity of being. Indeed, the analogicity of the being so perceived is so strong that from it one may causally infer the existence of God.

To be sure, the actual analogicity of being does not substitute either for the arguments showing that essence is really distinguished from existence (whereby it is clear that it is not merely because a thing has a material essence that it is, but because of its *actus essendi* that it is), nor for causal reasoning (whereby the truth of the proposition that God is, is affirmed). But the division of being into analogically diverse *rationes* of potency and act makes both the discovery of the real distinction of essence and existence, and the causal reasoning to the conclusion of God as pure act, to be possible. In fact, it provides the crucial evidence on the basis of which these proofs ascend to the conclusion that it is true that God exists, a conclusion rendered more profound by the real distinction of essence and existence. And one notes that in *De ente et essentia* the argument for real distinction of essence and existence is not predicated upon any demonstration of God in the physics. Neither does Aristotle anywhere in the *Metaphysics* condition metaphysical science on prior demonstrations of God in the physics—an odd thing to exclude from his introduction to the science if indeed it is a necessary condition of the existence of that science. But how could it be? Even when one may be unaware that physical substances are not the only things that are, they are affirmed to be analogically and by proper proportionality; and while the potency is really ordered to the act, act is as such not self-limiting. This, indeed, is precisely why only the discovery of *potentia* enables the reconciliation of the principle of noncontradiction with the data of many, limited, changing beings. Were being of itself self-limiting, there would no longer be any intelligible ground for the distinction of pure act and act limited by potency, of infinite and finite being, and it would strongly seem to imply that being as such need be finite. But just as being in no way denotes nonbeing, so being as such in no way denotes limit or plurifiability. One needs to see through to the very *ratio* of act as such, so as to see that change, motion, manyness, and limit all presuppose a principle that is neither nonbeing, nor mere possibility, but rather is founded upon actuality while really distinct from it, namely potency. It is largely the narrative of this formal metaphysical discovery that has been lost, not only in the negations of Suarez, but more principally in a certain slumber of forgetfulness with respect to the rigorous foundation of Aristotelian and Thomistic metaphysics.

In the heuristic order, the order of discovery, the ontology of nature or physics is prior to the metaphysics. But absolutely speaking, the subject matter of *ens commune* may be demonstrated to be actually and implicitly present from the start. For indeed, the "is" of the first way of the *Summa theologiae* is already intrinsically and actually analogous in the premises of that demonstration. (Else we would conclude to an unmoved *moved* mover, i.e., we would conclude to an "is" alloyed with potency because the being contained in the premises of the argument is merely material being and there cannot be in the conclusion that which is not in the premises.) But the sense of being as contained in the premises of the argument is already intrinsically and actually analogical. Here we already see that neither in being nor in notion or intention are perfections said in the same way of creature and of God.

So there is a real and indeed metaphysical ground why being is not itself a genus, i.e., because all its differentiae are included within being: this is a datum about being. And, after all, genus is an accident of the essential nature as it exists in intellectual intention, and—as Aquinas later develops far more extensively than Aristotle, who nonetheless seems to have seen the nub of the principle[8]— essence and existence are really distinct.

While the famed *pros hen* analogy (wherein things are denominated by virtue of their relation to something that is properly such, e.g. a medicine is called "healthy" as a cause of health in the proper subject of health, namely, the body) may pertain to substance in general inasmuch as everything is being by relation to substance, various substances nonetheless are said to be; and yet that sense of "being" is not that of either genus or species but is properly and fully analogical.[9] As one substance is to its being, so is another to its being, where one substance is not the other, nor is the being of the one the being of the other: analogy of proper proportionality or of being and intention.

Even if one wanted to affirm that substances are said to be by *pros hen* analogy with God,[10] being is actually and implicitly analogous prior to the proof for the existence of God. Indeed, what is not in the premises cannot be in the conclusion, and therefore if "being" means "material being" in the premises, then it must mean "material being" in the conclusion: but God is not reached as material being. Ergo "being" or "to be" or "is" in the premises of any demonstration for God is already contained in those premises as implicitly and actually analogous. Further, the categories seem to be not merely classificatory categories but modes of being.

If by metaphysics we refer to the whole science, embracing its causal resolution of being in the first cause of being as creator, then metaphysics of course requires advertence to God. But the science of metaphysics begins—as *De ente et essentia* begins—with the being common to substance and the categories. It is telling that in his only express introduction to this science, Thomas proceeds from the being common to substance and the categories without anywhere implying that the cognition of the being common to substance and the categories may be achieved only consequent upon the demonstration of God or of the positive immateriality of the soul.

With all this, we return to the proportional likeness of diverse *rationes* of act and potency, a doctrine immeasurably enriched by Thomas's development of the real distinction of essence and existence, which Aristotle at root saw[11] but did not similarly and intensively develop. For *esse* is act in relation to *essentia* as potency, and this distinction divides all finite substances. Indeed, in *De ente et essentia*, before Thomas demonstrates the existence of God on the basis of the distinction of essence and existence, he first proves the universality of this distinction by showing that if there were a case wherein essence and existence were identical, then there could only be one, because all the ways in which being is plurifiable presuppose *potentia*. By hypothesis, were there a case wherein essence were identical with existence, it would be pure act. The extent to which the real distinction of act and potency is foundational in Thomas's metaphysics becomes clearest when it is realized that this distinction is unfolded very early within the account of the real and as a condition of reconciling the understanding of the first principle of being and thought with the clear and intelligible evidence of our perception. Even in the work of Aristotle, the conclusion is that being is divided by act and potency.

> Our meaning can be seen in the particular cases by induction, and we must not seek a definition of everything but be content to grasp the analogy, that it is as that which is building is to that which is capable of building, and the waking to the sleeping, and that which is seeing to that which has its eyes shut but has sight, and that which has been shaped out of the matter to the matter, and that which has been wrought up to the unwrought. Let actuality be defined by one member of this antithesis, and the potential by the other. But all things are not said in the same sense to exist actually, but only by analogy—as A is in B or to B, C is in D or to D;

for some are as movement to potency, and the others as substance to some sort of matter. (*Meta.* 1048a35–1048b9.)

All things are not said in the same sense to exist actually, but only by analogy. This conclusion is of course applicable to all the diverse *rationes* of act—the diverse *rationes* of act being a function of *potentia*. Or, at the height of metaphysics, as one being is to its *actus essendi*, so is another to its *actus essendi*.

But how can being be analogical? Suppose there were but one being? Would not being then be univocal? No, because the being common to substance and the categories is susceptible of addition, unlike the being of God to which no perfection whatsoever may be added. Created being is susceptible to addition only inasmuch as being is analogically divisible by potency and act. Being is, and can be, and is and can be said, in many ways. As divided by act and potency, and as divisible by act and potency, being is analogical. To be sure, each act of being is proportioned by the divine intention and causality to the essential nature of that which God wills to be, and each creature is as a being indivisible from itself and enjoys transcendental unity. But the very distinction between substance and the categories is indeed expressable as a distinction within being and in terms of the analogy of proportionality. Hence, even one being with its accidents will require the analogy of proportionality; as all the more, of course, will multiple subjects of being.

The height of the real distinction of potency and act is of course reached in the realization of the real distinction of essence and existence, where existence is understood as *super*formal and as not self-limiting. (Cf. *ST*, I, q. 7, art. 1, resp.: "Illud autem quod est maxime formale omnium, est ipsum esse . . ." *Esse* is the "form of forms" and "perfection of perfections.") The positive judgment of existential act is a cognitive contact with the most perfect of acts, the act of being, which is limited only by virtue of its relation to potency and not by virtue of anything absolutely necessary to act as such: act does not of itself express to the mind any limit.[12] Nor can participation or causality be properly understood save in terms of the prior realization that act is limited in relation to potency and so that act is not self-limiting. The diverse grades of being which God ordains are diverse by virtue of the relation and proportion of act to potency. This of course does not in any way entail the temporal priority of potency to act, but only that in the order of perfection act is ontologically prior to, and limited by, the potency of which it is the act—reciprocal relation and consequent limitation do not require or imply temporal priority. Thus the actualization of a certain capacity for being is simultaneously limited by and to that capacity. This created limitation is a function of the divine intention that a being with a certain quidditative character should exist, because the quiddity is to actual existence as potency is to act—it pertains to the very nature of finite being itself.

In this work I deliberately do not take up the full consideration of the inspiration of Thomas's doctrine of participation inasmuch as my concern here is to show that this doctrine hinges upon the division of being by act and potency, because potency limits the participation in being and establishes the degree of remotion from the first cause. This is a function of the propositions that act is not self-limiting and that it is the contraction by potency that accounts for the limitation of act. I am aware, of course, of the argument of Fr. Norris Clarke[13] that the limitation of act by potency is derivative of the metaphysics of participation, which Thomas discovered through Neoplatonic sources. Without fully responding to this argument, it may be said here without any derogation of the inspiration of these sources, that the speculative argument in its own right pressed by Thomas is that act is not self-limiting, and that act is limited only in relation to potency. That is, for Thomas this is a function of deepened insight into the doctrine of the division of being by potency and act.

Further, I would concur with one critical observation of Jude Chua Soo Meng,[14] who observes that "infinite" can pertain to the unlimited imperfection/potentiality of matter as well as to positive ontological perfection. Citing *ST*, I, q. 7, art. 1, Meng argues that only if Thomas had posited the former as pertaining to pure act would it contradict the teaching of Aristotle. That is, Thomas's emphasis on the role of ontologically positive infinitude in the perfection of act does not lead to a denial that pure act is immutable or incorruptible or self-sufficient, but to a deepened appreciation of these truths.

Thomas's deepened analysis of the metaphysics of act and potency is wholly consistent with and perfects Aristotle's doctrine. This is so even on the supposition that only the infinitude of the indeterminate or potency was affirmed by Aristotle (and one may still have pause about this supposition, inasmuch as his response to Parmenides unfolds precisely in relation to the discovery of *potentia*, constituting an indirect affirmation of what in Thomas becomes quite direct and clear). But more importantly, Thomas's insight is the *sine qua non* of the metaphysical doctrine of participation, since without remotion from the first cause owing to the contraction of act in relation to potency, there are no grades of being. The inspiration for this deepened insight into the nature of act is of course arguably in significant part a function of Neoplatonic teaching.[15] But the crucial speculative point remains that it is the nature of the act/potency distinction itself as intelligible in proportionate being that founds the doctrine of participation for Thomas. And this foundation is implicit from the beginning in Aristotle's discovery of the division of being by act and potency, in particular in the discovery of potency as essential in reconciling our knowledge of the first principle of noncontradiction with our perception of many, limited, changing beings, thus answering the spectre of Parmenidean monism.

The peerless realism of Thomas's account of the first principles, which articulates these even more fully and adequately, should not divert minds from the simple datum that, *sans* potency, to speak of "grades of being" will imply that act is self-limiting. But if act is self-limiting, metaphysical explanation is at a stroke made impossible, for in that case there is no longer any principled account as to why the creature is ontologically inferior to God. Indeed, taken unequivocally, the idea that act is self-limiting should consistently imply that God is limited in perfection inasmuch as God is pure act. But while it is doubtless true that the proposition that "act is self-limiting" could be taken to mean only that every act is limited to being the act it is, this in no wise explains how act should come to be limited, since "act" as such does not include in its nature and definition "potency." This is *per se nota* to one who considers the real principle of act. Indeed, properly viewed, "act is not self-limiting" is another form of the judgment that being is not nonbeing: for what is designated by "act" includes no limitation but only perfection—act is no more potency or limit than it is non-act. Hence the Aristotelian answer to Parmenides is the necessary condition for any ontologically pluralist doctrine of participation (i.e., the doctrine of the Platonic forms does not sufficiently answer Parmenides), and the Thomistic maxim that act is not self-limiting is implied by and inflects this answer more perfectly, while it is implicitly and actually already contained within it. To show that it is contained within it, it suffices to consider well the nature and meaning of act, as well as the role of potency in answering Parmenidean monism.

Thomas clearly understands himself to be articulating the implications of the division of being by potency and act, and nowhere does he suggest that the judgment that act is not self-limiting is incompatible with the Aristotelian doctrine that being is divided by potency and act. In historical terms, surely we should give some priority to an author's own account of his undertaking. In speculative terms, however, we must be capable of distinguishing between the objective nature and implications of a principle and the awareness of these that a philosopher enjoys. Happily, in the present instance these two considerations converge: for Thomas both understands himself to be developing and explaining act and potency and explicitly shows us aspects of the doctrine that Aristotle deemphasized and was perhaps unaware of to some degree. In any case, I deem it false to say that the response to Parmenides in terms of the discovery of potency does not finally and objectively imply Thomas's maxim that act is not self-limiting. To the contrary, potency accounts for the susceptibility of being to limitation in perfection, change, and multiplicity. Clearly the Thomistic articulation involves a deeper penetration of the nature of this very doctrine. And Aristotle nowhere states that act as such includes in its nature or meaning any potency or imperfection, having limit only in the sense of determinacy—i.e., the determinacy of act itself. But the perfection of act itself is limited only in relation to potency, and lacks only that infinity signified by indetermination, potency, or matter.

In respect of the distinction of potency and act, Thomas's teaching that act is not self-limiting adds the final letter of a word yet already audibly spoken by Aristotle. This judgment requires metaphysical *scientia*, as it is not a function of projecting oneself into the individual consciousness of Aristotle. It is said that Einstein proved one of his relativity theorems a year before he realized it—the earlier written proof being found later in its completeness on a dated paper. It is not unusual for a mind to discover truths and not fully to realize the scope, nature, or implicational dynamism of that which has been discovered. The objective presence or absence of a truth is not a function merely of the individual consciousness of the theorist, but also of the nature of the truth discovered and its implications. So it is with the profundity of the division of being by act and potency, first discovered by Aristotle in the course of answering Parmenides and further (and most fully) appreciated and developed by Aquinas. There can be no doubt that in Thomas's teaching the division of being into act and potency is affirmed to be prior in reality to the grading of created effects as participating the divine causality; and that it is also prior in our knowledge (for remotion from the first cause is a function of the degree and kind of potency in relation to which act is limited). The motion in Thomas's work toward the realization that the doctrine of participation requires and is founded upon the division of being by act and potency is articulated clearly by Klubertanz. He traces the progress in Thomas's thought from *Scriptum super Sententiis*, where Thomas attributes the imperfection of participated perfection vaguely to "the recipient" of that perfection; on to his criticisms of participation in *De veritate*; and finally to his mature realization in *De potentia dei*, and even more clearly in the *Summa contra gentiles*, that the imperfection of the participated perfection is a function of its limitation by *potentia*.[16] With respect to this progress, Klubertanz argues:

We can conclude that the doctrine of participation underwent a development in the works of St. Thomas. In the early works it appears as a vague descriptive term, devoid of any profound metaphysical relations to the basic metaphysical principles of St. Thomas' thought. In its second stage, by being joined with the fully developed doctrine of act and potency, it is a clear, definite, and metaphysical doctrine.[17]

Klubertanz of course goes further, arguing in the same chapter:

Father Clarke, "Limitation of Act by Potency" (above, n. 11), considers this development to be a sign of the way in which St. Thomas became progressively more Platonic. Since this present study is not concerned with St. Thomas' sources, an alternative interpretation can be offered only in passing and as a suggestion. Perhaps St. Thomas began his treatment of the relation between God and the world mostly as a theologian, adopting the participation terminology from tradition as a tenable position; as he came to see its philosophical difficulties, he abandoned it; with a new philosophical insight that was compatible with other metaphysical principles, he developed *his own meaning* for the traditional terminology.[18]

Certainly the criticisms of participation in *De veritate*—and the free-floating character of the doctrine of participation vis-à-vis Thomas's own metaphysics prior to explanation of participation by the limitation of act by potency—support such a suggestion. In any case, from *De potentia dei* onwards, Thomas articulates the doctrine of participation in terms of the division of being by act and potency, and it is difficult to see either how this doctrine *could* be a Thomistic doctrine, or what evidentiary foundation whatsoever it might enjoy, were it not founded upon the division of being by act and potency. Of course it is also conspicuous that Thomas adverts to potency in *De ente et essentia* in arguing why if there were a being in whom essence and existence are identical, there could be but one such being; and the doctrine of essence (as potency) as really distinct from *esse* (as act) is most certainly the foundation for his metaphysics of participation.[19]

Far from being merely the hypostatization of Parmenidean monism into a "beyond," this reasoning—and even the earlier erroneous Parmenidean teaching—reflects something of the basic dialectic of act. Act is not self-limiting, and so pure act will necessarily transcend all limited act and indeed all limit of perfection. That this is implied by the evidence of finite being does not imply that *actus purus* is in itself known nor that it is merely the univocal "extension" of the perfection immanent to finite being (which is always proportioned to *potentia*). It does not place creature and God alike under a third principle called "being." (God does not fall under the being common to substance and the categories, but is rather its cause and principle.) Rather, it is to see that the perfection of finite act implies pure or infinite act, while seeing that nonetheless there is no determinate relation of pure act—of God—to the creature. Even the Parmenidean error approaches this insight, although it fails to address the evidence of the many, limited, changing beings. Hence it falls short of realizing the creature's real relation to God while in a spurious way upholding that God has no real relation to the creature; spurious because it denies the very reality of the creature.

Analogy of proper proportionality does not place creature and God indifferently under being, but rather affirms that the actuality of God is infinitely more perfect and nobler than that of the creature—or of all proportionate being—an excess that is not defined by any determinate quantum of perfection, but which exceeds all proportion. And why does it exceed all proportion to the creature and to created being, true, and good? Because it is wholly free of *potentia*, the proportion to which alone accounts for limitation in the perfection of being. If everything enjoys the perfection of being in limited proportion to its grade of being, and the grade of being is determined by diverse *rationes* of act which are such only because of *potentiae*, then any reality that is pure act wholly unlimited by any potency will infinitely surpass all creatures in its perfection in being (and truth and goodness). But this is analogy of proper proportionality once more, where indeed the limit case is the case wherein essence, while a measure of the perfection of being, is yet not a potential and thus limiting principle (because the essence is identical with existence). In such a case, the perfection must exceed any proportion to the creature, because the essence is not a limit to, but rather is identical with, pure act.

The answer to the question of why God is said to be pure being,[20] and to the question of why the perfection of being in God infinitely exceeds any proportion to the creature, is the same: in God there is no potency to limit the perfection of act, and act is not self-limiting. Thus, far from falling together with the creature under the *aegis* of a "neutral category" of being, God is Himself pure being, the causal origin of the creature infinitely exceeding the being of the creature. And the ground on the basis of which this reasoning to God occurs is precisely the being common to substance and the categories, which requires causal resolution into a principle that does not itself suffer limitation, manyness, and change. Our conclusion manifests and retains its formal relation to our starting place. It is no imperfection in God which accounts for this, but rather our own genuine but imperfect hold upon the real.

The onto-logic of the relation of potency to act as that of the determinable to the determined, and the perfectible to the perfect, passes deep into the fabric of Thomistic contemplation. And the ontological likeness of differing *rationes* of act and potency is the analogy of proportionate being. It is this that renders possible the causal reasoning concluding to the existence of God in every one of the proofs. Because the "is" of the premises is analogical, it accordingly does not violate the proportionate identity necessary for demonstration that the "is" of the conclusion be analogical.

Further, it is clear that while the creature is really related to God, God is not really related to the creature: the creature wholly depends on God, but God does not depend on the creature. Hence any speech about God cannot place God in a determined relation to the creature. Any analogy of proportion—even the analogy of cause to effect or of one to another—must, then, presuppose the absence of proportion in the strict sense of quantitative proportion or of placing God in a determinate relation to the creature. And the only way of achieving this is indeed to say that as the creature is to what is its own, so God is to what is His own; as the creature is to its act, so is God to His act. For while what is affirmed is perfection in each case, the meaning and being of the perfection differ and differ infinitely; the meaning and being of perfection in God is without any limit of potentiality, while the meaning and being of perfection in the creature involves limit of potentiality. Once this is understood, then—because the creature truly is ordered to God—an improper or general analogy of proportion as when anything is related to anything else, of one to another, may be affirmed; as, likewise, analogy of effect to cause. But this improper analogy of proportion must be translatable into analogy of proper proportionality, because otherwise one is placing God into a determined relation to the creature, which is simply incompossible with the proposition of the transcendence and simplicity of God.

The truth that being is divided by act and potency, and that the analogy of being is analogy of proper proportionality, enables the causal reasoning of the theistic proofs to conclude licitly because the "is" of the premises is analogical, enabling the proportionate "is" of the conclusion. Further, this analogy enables one to make analogical affirmations regarding God for this same reason, as analogy of proper proportionality does not place God into a determined relation to the creature, while yet being consistent with the causal recognition that the creature is really related to God. It therefore permits a secondary and improper analogy of proportion between creature and God, which is always founded upon proper proportionality, precisely because it is not properly an analogy of proportion in the determinate sense. Yet this does not keep analogy of one to another, or of effect to cause, from being in an improper and transferred sense an analogy of proportion provided that one keep this in mind. It is this teaching, we shall see, that Thomas offers early in his writings and which his later writings, which focus on improper analogy of proportion, nonetheless never renounce.

Proceeding from the analogy of being that affords the evidence for this causal motion, once one reasons to the truth of the proposition that God exists, there is then a return motion of consideration in which one reframes one's awareness of the being common to substance and the categories as a gift, and as participated being derived from the unparticipated divine being. But these very insights presuppose and deploy the analogy of proper proportionality, for the way in which God is "being" is precisely as "unparticipated" *actus purus*, as infinitely exceeding created being as its source, such that here alone is being said to be unlimited in relation to *potentia*. This insight enables us to affirm that the transcendental and pure perfections of being are found without any proportion to finite being, with no limit of potency, such that it is truer to say that these perfections are in God than that they are in creatures. Yet we have no direct knowledge of divine perfection, but only a knowledge mediated through *creaturae* and through grace: the inference to God does not give us direct knowledge of God Himself, for were we to see God through these inferences we would already possess beatific vision.

The creature is really related to God. Things that are not their being, but receive their being from without, depend upon the gift of being from the One Who alone and fully *is*; things that move from potency to act depend upon the One Who alone is pure act; things that are effects depend upon the first cause; things that are contingent, or that have only hypothetic necessity, depend upon absolutely necessary being; limited perfection implies maximal or absolute perfection, for perfection (act) is not self-limiting; and the saturative actual ordering of nonrational creatures to their perfections requires absolutely ordering intelligence. Yet as all these conclusions take wing from the actual evidence of pluriform, limited, changing being, they always bear within them the signs of their origin.

The realization that created being is a gift derived from God, in Whom being is found infinitely exceeding all created limit, gives us the analogy of cause to effect, of one to another, of source to beneficiary. Yet these insights must—precisely because they do not gain entry into the divine essence, but give us true propositions about a divine essence known as unknown—still be expressable within, and presuppose, analogy of proper proportionality.

The proposition here is not the Maimonidean agnosis. It is true that transcendental and pure perfections are more properly said of God than of creature, because they are found in God without any limit of *potentia*, whereas in creatures they are always limited by *potentia*. But knowing the truth of this proposition so that we may say, "God is Being, God is Truth, God is Goodness," does not entail that the mind directly sees the infinite being, truth, and good Who is God. The knowledge of the truth of these propositions remains veiled in the epistemic limits of the created evidence which gives rise to this knowledge.

Yet the causal knowledge of God and the ensuing doctrine of participated and unparticipated being perfect our wisdom regarding the analogy of being inasmuch as the relative transcendence of the intrinsically analogical being common to substance and the categories implies the absolute transcendence of God. We may thus refer to the truths of the causal doctrine of participation as in a sense constituting analogous discourse about God, on the provision that we understand that this language is not self-standing, but is derived, and derived precisely through inference proceeding from the being analogically common to substance and the categories, whose stamp is always carried by our knowledge of these truths. Likewise, the analogy of being is no substitute for the causal reasoning that moves from limited to unlimited act but rather affords us a grasp of the real principles inviting and requiring such causal reasoning. But the conclusions of each of these reasonings, whether in the argument expressly proceeding from the real distinction of essence and existence, or in the five ways, presupposes and likewise always carries the stamp of the knowledge of proportionate being, a proportionate being analogous according to the likeness of diverse *rationes* of act (which is to say, diverse *rationes* of act and potency, since only the latter introduces plurifiability into being).[21] We know God as the One in Whom the utter fulness of every transcendental and pure perfection exists as identified with God's infinitely simple being—but the God thus surpassing all limit of potency is not known to us directly, but rather in this life is known only through causal reasoning proceeding from, and articulated in terms of, the analogy of being.

As both the proof for the existence of God and the doctrine of participation proceed from the foundation of the division of proportionate being by potency and act, neither can climb outside its own skin and actually vouchsafe to us a direct and unmediated intellection of God in Himself. Hence even the highest deliverances of causal reasoning, and of the doctrine of participation, are founded in the analogy of being as the likeness of diverse *rationes* of act and potency. For the doctrine of participation sets forth from diverse *rationes* of act which are diverse only owing to *potentiae*, and the inference to God likewise sets forth from the same evidence; these give us a knowledge of God as unknown, as the One in Whom pure act suffers no limit whatsoever and from Whom all limited being derives and upon Whom it depends. But this knowledge *about* God does not lift us to the direct knowledge of God. It is not beatitude. One recollects the poetic closing words of Jacques Maritain in *Existence and the Existent*.

> And now, if it is true that philosophy tends to go beyond itself in order to attain to the silence of unity, where it will harvest all that it knows in a purer and more transparent light, what is the experience in which it (whose first object is the world and man) can cause the spirit of man thus to expand, unless it be the experience of the gift of knowledge? Then will man attain peace, then will he be able to say, *ecce in pace amaritudo mea amarissima*. What the gift of knowledge produces, according to John of St. Thomas, is a certain experience or a *taste* of creatures which detaches us from them, a spiritual experience of created being which induces in us a yearning for God. "Thou art the Lord our God. In very deed the hills were liars, and the multitude of the moutains. Behold, we come to thee . . ." To what truer knowledge can the philosopher lay claim? He will have received his due when, one day, not by the discourse of reason but by a simple and intimate experience—in which all seems said, and in which compassion is made one with detachment—he will know that beings, with all their beauty, differ from the infinite Being more than they resemble Him. When he will know how great is the abandonment of those who, to hold the

created being within reach, were forced to scale the glaciers of the void where they see everywhere the void. When he will know that there is nothing more despised and rejected among men than the truth he loves, and will feel that for that truth every opportunity is a lost opportunity, and that its highest messages, if they are purely human, influence history only as a nudge to the blind and only when they can no longer be deciphered. When he will discern the irrefutable meaning of the *mihi videtur ut palea* and perceive that all that men have said about being and God must seem to the saints like a bundle of straw, and that the wisp which each man strives with so much labor to add to the bundle will not serve him, for it is according to his love that he will be judged. When he will understand that all the treasures of the intelligibility of being, all the glory of the *act of existing*, and the savour of the existent which he so much wished to taste, have always regarded him with infinite indifference and never wished to give themselves to him. For it was he who, by the law of the human intellect focusing its light upon the booty of the senses, had sought to seize those treasures by piercing the veil for a single instant. Therefore from the beginning he accepted disappointment, for we incur inevitable disappointment when we seek to take that which refuses to give itself. The hills may have been liars, but it was not the hills that disappointed him. One day the hills will surrender themselves, everything will surrender itself to the intelligence of man on the day when the self-subsistent *Act of Existing* shall give Itself in vison.[22]

St. Thomas on *Analogia Entis* in the *Scriptum super Sententiis* and in *De Veritate*

There are of course two famous loci *at which Thomas* articulates the analogy of being principally in terms of the analogy of proper proportionality, namely, the *Scriptum super Sententiis* and *De veritate*. In the latter work, the emphasis shifts to the way in which the analogy of proper proportionality enables speech about God without placing God in a determinate relation with a finite creature and so finitizing God; whereas in the former the relation to God anchors an emphasis upon the intrinsically analogous character of objects such as being, true, good, act, potency, substance, and so on, which are found in diverse perfection not only among creatures, but most radically as between God and creatures. Before briefly indicating why I think the contemporary retreat from this account of the *analogia entis* is not well-founded, a look at these two texts and their doctrine is helpful. This accordingly can afford us the occasion to make the turn from analogical discourse regarding God in general, to the heart of the analogical intelligibility of the act of faith itself.

In I, d. 19, q. 5, art. 2, ad 1 of his *Scriptum super Sententiis* Thomas speaks of three different types of analogy:[1]

> . . . it is to be said that something is said according to analogy in three ways [aliquid dicitur secundum analogiam tripliciter]: either according to notion only and not according to being [secundum intentionem tantum et non secundum esse]: and this is when one notion [una intentio] is referred to several [things] through priority and posteriority, which nevertheless has being only in one: for example, the notion of health [intentio sanitatis] is referred to the animal, the urine, and the diet in diverse measures [diversimode], according to priority and posteriority; not nevertheless according to diverse being, because the being of health is only in the animal.
>
> Or else, [something is said according to analogy] according to being and not according to notion [secundum esse et non secundum intentionem]; and this occurs when many things are taken as equal [parificantur] in the notion [in intentione] of something common, but that common item does not have being of one intelligible character [esse unius rationis] in all: as for example, all bodies are taken as equal in the notion of corporeity [in intentione corporeitatis]; hence, the logician [logicus], who considers only notions [intentiones tantum], says that this name "body" is predicated of all bodies univocally; however, the being of this nature [esse hujus naturae] is not of the same intelligible character [ejusdem rationis] in corruptible and incorruptible bodies; hence, for the metaphysician and the physicist, who consider things according to their being, neither this name, "body," nor any other [name] is said univocally of corruptibles and incorruptibles, as is clear from *Metaph.* 10, text 5, from [both] the Philosopher and the Commentator.
>
> Or else, [something is said according to analogy] according to notion and according to being [secundum intentionem et secundum esse], and this is when they are not taken as equal either in the

common notion [in intentione communi] or in being; the way, for example, "a being" is said of substance and accident; and in such [cases] it is necessary that the common nature [natura communis] have some being in each of those things of which it is said, but differing according to the [measure] intelligible character [rationem] of greater or lesser perfection.

And similarly I say [dico] that "truth" and "goodness" and all such [items] are said analogically [dicuntur analogice] of God and creatures. Hence, it is necessary that according to their being all these be in God and in creatures according to the measure/ intelligible character [secundum rationem] of greater and lesser perfection; from which it follows, since they cannot be according to one being [esse] in both places, that there are diverse truths [diversae veritates].

It is difficult to deny that, at least here, Thomas identifies the first or *pros hen* analogy as that of extrinsic attribution, for health does not exist in the medicine, for example, but only in the animal. Thus the notion/intention is analogical, but the being of health is not, because it isn't genuinely found in medicine; rather, medicine is understood to be "healthy" merely as a cause of health.

The second analogy—that of being but not of notion/intention— is illustrated by "body" as univocal for the logician, but as analogical for the metaphysician or physicist insofar as the heavenly bodies are incorruptible in Aristotelian physics but sublunary bodies are corruptible. Hence inasmuch as "body" is found in two drastically diverse manners and with a radically different ontological perfection in incorruptible and corruptible bodies, it would follow that the common logical notion "body" would not adequately measure their difference which is known to the scientific understanding, for this difference pertains to reality as such and not merely to the logical categorization.

It is in the third instance of analogy—that according to notion/ intention and according to being (*secundum intentionem et secundum esse*)—that it appears one finds a doctrine of real analogy according to proper proportionality.

... "truth" and "goodness" and all such [items] are said analogically [dicuntur analogice] of God and creatures. Hence, it is necessary that according to their being all these be in God and in creatures according to the [measure] intelligible character [secundum rationem] of greater and lesser perfection; from which it follows, since they cannot be according to one being [esse] in both places, that there are diverse truths [diversae veritates].

Clearly, the perfections spoken of God and creatures do not have the same being as between God and creatures, nor accordingly is their truth the same. That is, "it is necessary that according to their being all these be in God and in creatures according to the measure/ intelligible character of greater and lesser perfection; from which it follows, since they cannot be according to one being in both places, that there are diverse truths." But to speak of greater or lesser perfection, both in being and in notion, is to speak of a likeness of *diverse rationes* of act (i.e., perfection is act, whether existential act, formal act, operative act, etc.)—for the diversity is in both being and notion, but there is indeed likeness of the diverse measures of perfection. The real analogy in this case is not purely equivocal because there is a likeness in the differing *rationes* of perfection in God and creatures (differing both in being and in concept). But neither is it univocal: this perfection neither exists in the same way, nor is it understood as simply the same, because the *ratio* of perfection differs in each. Only God is pure act, *ipsum esse subsistens per se*, and we know God as not knowing Him inasmuch as we do not know the way in which all the intelligible perfections affirmed of God exist as identified with the simple divine substance. We cannot help recollecting this proposition when we are told that being and truth and all such objects are analogical not only with respect to notion or intention, but also with respect to being. This is certainly the case when we read in *ST*, I, q. 13, art. 5, ad 1, that "all univocal predications are reduced to one first non-univocal analogical predication, which is being." For might it not be that both in notion and in being, the analogy of being is a likeness of differing *rationes* of act and potency? If for a creature to be is for it to be a subject of being with an essential nature, and to receive the act of being, and to stand in relation to that act as potency, then the analogy of being is the likeness in difference of varying modes of being. Further, inasmuch as finite things are beings, being is said of them by intrinsic and not extrinsic predication: indeed, if finite being does not exist, there can be no proof for the existence of God. But the analogy of proper proportionality is an analogy of intrinsic attribution: being is said of each analogate intriniscally, for each exists (unlike the case, say, of medicine in *pros hen* analogy, which is said to be healthy owing to its relation to the body, which is the proper subject of health, rather than by intrinsic attribution). Accordingly, it appears that the analogy of being requires proper proportionality (the angel is to its *esse* as the whale is to its *esse*, but the *esse* of one is not that of the other, and the angel is not a whale). It is upon the evidence of this being that is common to substance and the categories and divided by act and potency that causal reasoning mounts to the conclusion that God, pure act, transcending *ens commune* as its cause, exists.

De veritate, q. 2, art. 11, "Is Knowledge Predicated of God and Men Purely Equivocally?" is even more clear:

> It is impossible to say that something is predicated univocally of a creature and God because in all univocal predication the nature signified by the name is common to those of whom the univocal predication is made. Hence, from the point of view of the nature signified by the predicate, the subjects of the univocal predication are equal, even though from the point of view of its real existence one may take precedence over another. For example, all numbers are equal from the point of view of the nature of number, even though, by the nature of things, one number is naturally prior to another. No matter how much a creature imitates God, however, a point cannot be reached where something would belong to it for the same reason it belongs to God. For things which have the same formal characters but are in separate subjects are common to the same subjects in regard to substance or quiddity but distinct in regard to the act of being. But whatever is in God is His own act

of being; and just as His essence is the same as His act of being, so is His knowledge the same as His act of being a knower. Hence, since the act of existence proper to one thing cannot be communicated to another, it is impossible that a creature ever attain to the possession of something in the same manner in which God has it, just as it is impossible for it to attain the same act of being as that which God has. The same is true of us. If man and to exist as man did not differ in Socrates, man could not be predicated univocally of him and Plato, whose acts of existing are distinct.

Nevertheless, it cannot be said that whatever is predicated of God and creatures is an equivocal predication; for, unless there were at least some real agreement between creatures and God, His essence would not be the likeness of creatures, and so He could not know them by knowing His essence. Similarly, we would not be able to attain any knowledge of God from creatures, nor from among the names devised for creatures could we apply one to Him more than another; for in equivocal predication it makes no difference what name is used, since the word does not signify any real agreement.

Consequently, it must be said that knowledge is predicated neither entirely univocally nor yet purely equivocally of God's knowledge and ours. Instead, it is predicated analogously, or, in other words, according to a proportion. Since an agreement according to proportion can happen in two ways, two kinds of community can be noted in analogy. There is a certain agreement between things having a proportion to each other from the fact that they have a determinate distance between each other or some other relation to each other, like the proportion which the number two has to unity in as far as it is the double of unity. Again, the agreement is occasionally noted not between two things which have a proportion between them, but rather between two related proportions—for example, six has something in common with four because six is two times three, just as four is two times two. The first type of agreement is one of proportion; the second, of proportionality.

We find something predicated analogously of two realities according to the first type of agreement when one of them has a relation to the other, as when being is predicated of substance and accident because of the relation which accident has to substance, or as when healthy is predicated of urine and animal because urine has some relation to the health of an animal. Sometimes, however, a thing is predicated analogously according to the second type of agreement, as when sight is predicated of bodily sight and of the intellect because understanding is in the mind as sight is in the eye.

In those terms predicated according to the first type of analogy, there must be some definite relation between the things having something in common analogously. Consequently, nothing can be predicated analogously of God and creature according to this type of analogy; for no creature has such a relation to God that it could determine the divine perfection. But in the other type of analogy, no definite relation is involved between the things which have something in common analogously, so there is no reason why some name cannot be predicated analogously of God and creature in this manner.

But this can happen in two ways. Sometimes the name implies something belonging to the thing primarily designated which cannot be common to God and creature even in the manner described above. This would be true, for example, of anything predicated of God metaphorically, as when God is called lion, sun, and the like, because their definition includes matter which cannot be attributed to God. At other times, however, a term predicated of God and creature implies nothing in its principal meaning which would prevent our finding between a creature and God an agreement of the type described above. To this kind belong all attributes which include no defect nor depend on matter for their act of existence, for example, being, the good, and similar things.[2]

It is in this much disdained writing that Thomas expressly answers the question how it is that analogical predication of "attributes which include no defect nor depend on matter for their act of existence, for example, being, the good, and similar things" can avoid placing God into a determined relation to the creature—what one may take to be the Barthian objection to analogy. Indeed, the sympathy for what we may construe to be Barth's concern is very formal: "No matter how much a creature imitates God, however, a point cannot be reached where something would belong to it for the same reason it belongs to God." The last four paragraphs quoted above constitute his one specific answer to this concern which he nowhere later expressly repudiates or negates.

Of the two types of analogy of proportion, the first presupposes determinate relation among the subjects sharing analogically in some perfection; of the second type, "as when sight is predicated of bodily sight and of the intellect because understanding is in the mind as sight is in the eye," Thomas states that "no definite relation is involved between the things which have something in common analogously, so there is no reason why some name cannot be predicated analogously of God and creature in this manner." Describing these two types of analogy, one of proportion and the other of proportionality, which alone can permit analogous predication of God and creature, he makes clear that the first involves things that "have a determinate distance between each other or some other relation to each other," whereas the second pertains not to two things but rather to "two related proportions," as "for example six has something in common with four because six is two times three, just as four is two times two." Mathematically speaking, six is to three precisely as four is to two, i.e., "double," which is indeed a univocal object. This mathematical usage—which is admirable as a beginning—soon gives way, however, to genuine analogy: "Sometimes, however, a thing is predicated analogously according to the second type of agreement, as when sight is predicated of bodily sight and of the intellect because understanding is in the mind as sight is in the eye." This is genuinely analogical, because bodily vision is not intellectual vision, nor is the intellect a body, and yet there is a likeness of diverse *rationes*.

Further, and to make things very clear, Thomas writes:

> In those terms predicated according to the first type of analogy, there must be some definite relation between the things having something in common analogously. Consequently, nothing can

be predicated analogously of God and creature according to this type of analogy; for no creature has such a relation to God that it could determine the divine perfection. But in the other type of analogy, no definite relation is involved between the things which have something in common analogously, so there is no reason why some name cannot be predicated analogously of God and creature in this manner.

Nothing can be predicated analogously of God and creature by proportion because "no creature has such a relation to God that it could determine the divine perfection." This is not an inadvertent, offhand, or desultory proposition, but a fully discriminate one. Thomas is denying that any finite perfection as such can have a proportion directly to God. The reason is that God transcends the proportion of all finite being, and vis-à-vis any species and in terms of its specific perfection is an equivocal cause of it, because God stands within no genus or species, and transcends all genera. If we say that there is a proportion of creaturely perfection to God, it seems that we are saying that between created perfection and God there may be found a determinate distance, as for example we find in the analogy of proportion whereby the number two is analogous to one and is related thereto as its double. But the divine perfection indefinitely exceeds any such determinate relation to a created finite perfection. Only inasmuch as "no definite relation is involved between the things which have something in common analogously" is it the case that "there is no reason why some name cannot be predicated analogously of God and creature in this manner"—i.e., when we are speaking of the likeness of diverse *rationes* which do not fall within a determinate univocal order. There is not utter equivocation between God and creature, else as Thomas says regarding the divine essence:

> . . . for, unless there were at least some real agreement between creatures and God, His essence would not be the likeness of creatures, and so He could not know them by knowing His essence. Similarly, we would not be able to attain any knowledge of God

from creatures, nor from among the names devised for creatures could we apply one to Him more than another . . .

Of course it is the case that we must distinguish proper analogical speech from metaphorical speech about God where what is principally designated by the analogical term cannot be predicated of God (God as a lion, or as a stone, etc.). But there is strictly analogous speech regarding God and creatures:

> At other times, however, a term predicated of God and creature implies nothing in its principal meaning which would prevent our finding between a creature and God an agreement of the type described above. To this kind belong all attributes which include no defect nor depend on matter for their act of existence, for example, being, the good, and similar things.

Why, then, can being or good be predicated analogously of God? Because being is perfection in creatures, and being is perfection in God. As God is not the creature, so the utter perfection of God's being is not the perfection of being in the creature. But there is a likeness inasmuch as the very name of God is Being, "I Am Who Am," such that the full perfection of being is more properly affirmed of God than of any creature. Do we know the perfection thereby attributed to God as it is in truth identified with the infinitely simple and perfect divine essence and being? No. But we know the truth *that* God Is, and that this "Is" is limited by no potency whatsoever, unlike the "is" of creatures. The perfection of act is not self-limiting, but only limited by potency. As we know how it is that potency analogically limits, and as we have causal analysis that requires us to conclude to the first cause as pure act, we know that every pure perfection (having a "floor" but no "ceiling"—e.g., wisdom) and transcendental perfection (found wherever there is being) must pertain radically and comprehensively to God in a mode (without any limit of potency) of which we have no direct knowledge.

The analogy of being does not perform our causal reasoning for us. Yet the analogy of being enables us to see that as the being common to substance and the categories is divided by act and potency, the existential act of each being must resolve into pure act; and it also enables us to see that the being common to substance and the categories must offer some limited likeness to its divine proper cause. Ascetically remove all limit of potentiality from every pure or transcendental perfection, and in that way, with no such limit, the perfections subsist as identified within the divine essence. But we do not have direct knowledge of them as identified with the divine substance in this way, but only as they are found limited by potency in creatures. Hence our knowledge is not knowledge of God's essence, but as it were true knowledge "about" God's essence, for the truth of the human proposition that every pure or transcendental perfection belongs infinitely to God with no limit of potency whatsoever is not tantamount to the beatific vision. This does not mean that our statements are false. It means that the divine truth infinitely transcends the truth about God that we can cognize through human propositions.

The diverse *rationes* of act common to substance and the categories thus, as limited, have some likeness to God, but are more unlike, because infinite act with no limit of potency is infinitely unlike finite being. Yet because it is indeed the transcendental and pure perfections that are in God without limit and as identified with His simple being, there is a certain likeness to God in creatures that goes along with an even greater unlikeness. As Thomas puts it in *De veritate*, q. 2, art. 11, ad 1:

> As Dionysius says, God can in no way be said to be similar to creatures, but creatures can in some sense be said to be similar to Him. For what is made in imitation of something, if it imitates it perfectly, can be said to be like it absolutely. But however the opposite is not true; because a man is not said to be similar to his image but the converse. But if the imitation is imperfect, then it is said to be both like and unlike that which it imitates: like insofar as it resembles it; unlike insofar as it falls short of a perfect representation. Thus it is for this reason that sacred scripture denies that creatures are similar to God in every way. It does sometimes grant

that creatures are like God and sometimes denies this. It concedes the similarity when it says that man is made in the likeness of God, but negates it when it is said in the Psalms, "O God Who is like unto thee?"[3]

In *De veritate*, q. 23, art. 7, ad 9, Thomas makes very clear the sense of this analogy of proper proportionality, while also affirming that any analogy of one to another presupposes it. He writes:

> Man is conformed to God since he is made to God's image and likeness. It is true that, because man is infinitely distant from God, there cannot be proportion between him and God in the proper sense of proportion as found among quantities, consisting of a certain measure of two quantities compared to each other. *Nevertheless, in the sense in which the term proportion is transferred to signify any relationship of one thing to another (as we say that there is a likeness of proportions in this instance: the pilot is to his ship as the ruler to the commonwealth), nothing prevents us saying that there is a proportion of man to God, since man stands in a certain relationship to Him inasmuch as he is made by God and subject to Him.* [Emphasis mine.]
>
> Or it could be said that although there cannot be between the finite and the infinite a proportion properly so called, still there can be proportionality which is the likeness of two proportions. We say that four is proportioned to two because it is the double; but we say that four is proportionable to six because four is to two as six is to three. In the same way, although the finite and the infinite cannot be proportioned, they can be proportionable, because the finite is equal to the finite, just as the infinite is to the infinite. In this way there is a likeness of the creature to God, because the creature stands to the things which are its own as God does to those which belong to Him.[4]

Here too we see the insistence that there cannot be a determined relation of God to man. Yet there is a determined relation of man to God (man is made in the image and likeness of God) and in the general sense of analogy of one to another, this improper sense of "proportion" may be understood in terms of the analogy of proper proportionality or the likeness of diverse proportions "as we say that there is a likeness of proportions in this instance: the pilot is to his ship as the ruler to the commonwealth" and "because the creature stands to the things which are its own as God does to those which belong to Him." Here again we see the ontological proportioning of act to the subject of act which is not merely predicative but metaphysical. In God there is no potency whereby the perfection of act is limited—God is identical with the fullness of the perfection of being—whereas in the creature act is limited by potency—the creature is not its being.[5] Yet act is, proportionate to the subject, perfection in each, although by reason of created limit we cannot cognize the divine perfection in itself which exceeds all created analogates.

All this is a function of the *analogia entis* understood as the likeness of diverse *rationes* of potency and act, and of the dialectic of act so understood and its causal analysis. Pure act is like act that is limited by potency in being perfection, but it is more unlike it because the perfection in God is infinite and not limited, and no created perfection can adequately represent unlimited perfection because created perfection is limited by potency and finite. Thus does the analogy of being, as entering into causal analysis (as in the proofs), enable the judgment both whereby the utter aseity and transcendence of God is affirmed, and whereby the limited likeness of the creature with its feeble share of the perfection of *esse* limited by potency is similar to the one who is *ipsum esse subsistens per se*. And indeed this purely philosophic instrumentality articulates in its way the teaching of the Fourth Lateran Council in 1215 AD— for "between the Creator and the creature so great a likeness cannot be noted without the necessity of noting a greater dissimilarity between them."[6]

Consideration of Objections to the View That the *Analogia Entis* Is the Analogy of Proper Proportionality

The objections to the proposition that the analogia entis is correctly understood as analogy of proper proportionality according to the likeness of diverse *rationes* of act and potency—most centrally, according to diverse *rationes* of the *actus essendi*, the act of being, and essence as limiting potential principle—are legion. Within the present confines it is in principle impossible to offer materially sufficient reply to each of the essential objections that has been raised to this reading of Thomas and Aristotle. Nonetheless we may identify and respond to certain most formal and principal objections before turning to the essential implication of the intelligibility of the analogy of being for that of the act of faith.

The Historical Objection

The most common objection to defining the analogy of being as the analogy of proper proportionality asserts that this was merely a marginal and early view that Aquinas later discarded without regret or notice later in his work—a teaching to be replaced by analogy of proportion or of one to another. Indeed, nowhere in his later writing does Thomas expressly offer the arguments we have cited from *De veritate* and from the *Scriptum super Sententiis*. And Thomas does speak of analogy in later works. As Klubertanz puts it, referring to the passages in *De veritate* where Thomas insists upon analogy of proper proportionality:[1]

> Here we merely wish to point out an item of chronological interest: these proportionality texts were both written about the year 1256–1257. There are no later texts mentioning proper proportionality in the discussions of the analogy between God and creatures. This fact seems to indicate a definite doctrinal change—we shall have to examine the precise bearing of this point later. We wish only to mention here that as he did with the formal exemplarity of the divine ideas, St. Thomas abandoned explicit proportionality in his later writings as the only description of the analogy between God and creatures.[2]

Likewise, Klubertanz argues:

> For a period of some months around 1256, St. Thomas either held or considered holding proper proportionality as *the* intrinsic analogy explaining the ontological similarity between God and creatures. This position he had not held previously and would never develop again in subsequent writings. Proper proportionality is therefore a Thomistic analogy in the sense that it is a doctrine taught by St. Thomas for a brief period early in his career.[3]

Is it not then clear that Thomas abandoned these early positions? One might conclude so if one thought either that the teachings in question are proposed merely as possibilities or as marginal articulations of his views, or else if one thought that Thomas were the type of author who would utterly reject earlier central teachings without giving an account of the reasons for such rejection. But if that is not the case, and if these teachings are not marginal, then this conclusion seems very unlikely to be true.

Are the teachings mere marginal expressions of possibilities? It is true that in the disputed questions Thomas explores various possibilities, but the argument we have cited directly above is not in a provisional mode. As between analogy of proportion and analogy of proportionality:

> In those terms predicated according to the first type of analogy, there must be some definite relation between the things having something in common analogously. Consequently, nothing can be predicated analogously of God and creature according to this type of analogy; for no creature has such a relation to God that it could determine the divine perfection. But in the other type of analogy, no definite relation is involved between the things which have something in common analogously, so there is no reason why some name cannot be predicated analogously of God and creature in this manner. (*De veritate*, q. 2, article 11)

The "other type of analogy" is, for example, "as when sight is predicated of bodily sight and of the intellect because understanding is in the mind as sight is in the eye," and to this type of analogy "belong all attributes which include no defect nor depend on matter for their act of existence, for example, being, the good, and similar things."

Hence we see that the analogy of being and good belong to proper proportionality. This is not a teaching that by the remotest stretch of the imagination can be characterized as marginal, or one that is put forward as a mere possibility. The text does not support such a frivolous reading. If this doctrine occurred solely in *De veritate*, the question would still need to be asked: is this doctrine *anywhere* expressly repudiated or denied in Thomas's later writing? The

answer to this question is: *no*. And so it is at least possible to conclude that while Thomas never again raised the question precisely
as he addressed it in *De veritate*, he also never altered his answer to
that question, but elaborated around it.[4] It may also be said that the
Summa theologiae considers these questions differently, although in
a way suggestive of the need for the earlier teaching. For instance,
in *ST*, I, q. 13, art. 9, ad 3, we find:

> These names "good," "wise," and the like, are imposed from the
> perfections proceeding from God to creatures; but they do not
> signify the divine nature, but rather signify the perfections them-
> selves absolutely; and therefore they are in truth communicable to
> many. But this name "God" is given to God from His own proper
> operation, which we experience continually, to signify the divine
> nature.[5]

Here again we find the view of analogous perfections as "in truth
communicable to many"—clearly, the ontological *rationes* whereby
these perfections are communicated will be comparable while diverse. But there is no express reiteration of the analogy of proper
proportionality in a way similar to that of *De veritate*.

In *ST*, I, q. 13, art. 5, we find a teaching that seems absolutely
to imply the need for the doctrine of proper proportionality. In this
passage, the analogy of God and creatures is addressed from the
vantage point of the purification/negation of the created mode of
the perfections predicated of God. Thomas argues that the affirmation of these perfections *sans* their created limits is such that
God is incomprehended by and exceeds such perfections. God possesses in simple unity the pure perfections that in creatures exist
multiply, separately, and with limit. Indeed, Thomas articulates a
causal ground as to why our understanding of the analogical term
predicated of God cannot comprehend or circumscribe the divine
perfection. To cite the passage:

> Univocal predication is impossible between God and creatures.
> The reason of this is that every effect which is not an adequate

result of the power of the efficient cause, receives the similitude of the agent not in its full degree, but in a measure that falls short, so that what is divided and multiplied in the effects resides in the agent simply, and in the same manner; as for example the sun by exercise of its one power produces manifold and various forms in all inferior things. In the same way, as said in the preceding article, all perfections existing in creatures divided and multiplied, pre-exist in God unitedly. Thus when any term expressing perfection is applied to a creature, it signifies that perfection distinct in idea from other perfections; as, for instance, by the term "wise" applied to man, we signify some perfection distinct from a man's essence, and distinct from his power and existence, and from all similar things; whereas when we apply to it God, we do not mean to signify anything distinct from His essence, or power, or existence. Thus also this term "wise" applied to man in some degree circumscribes and comprehends the thing signified; whereas this is not the case when it is applied to God; but it leaves the thing signified as incomprehended, and as exceeding the signification of the name. Hence it is evident that this term "wise" is not applied in the same way to God and to man. The same rule applies to other terms. Hence no name is predicated univocally of God and of creatures.[6]

Yet what is the need articulated in *De veritate* for analogy of proper proportionality in respect to created and divine perfections? What is the *reason* given by *De veritate* that only an improper and "transferred" sense of analogy of proportion as of any relation of one thing to another, but precisely *not* any quantitative proportion or proportion placing God in a determined relation to the creature, is possible? Is the reason not precisely that both in being and in notion, analogical perfection varies as between creature and God— and varies precisely by reason of the absolute transcendence and simplicity of God, Who has no determined relation to the creature and thus cannot be placed in any determinate relation to the creature? Is this not precisely what is affirmed in making clear that the analogical perfection as said of God leaves what is signified not only "as incomprehended, and as exceeding the signification of the name," but moreover as "exceeding the signification of the name" *not* by any fixed proportion? What, then, is the proportion with which the perfection is found? While it is proportionate to God as to one in whom perfection is found utterly unlimited by potency, God cannot be put into any determinate relation to the creature, although the creature is determined in relation to God. To use the language of *De veritate* in q. 23, art. 7, ad 9, "the creature stands to the things which are its own as God does to those which belong to Him." We know that the divine perfection infinitely exceeds the finite; we cannot, however, claim that this "exceeding" is by fixed proportion, because of the divine simplicity and transcendence. While the emphasis on analogy of proportion, of one to another, and of effect to cause are all to be found in Thomas's later writings, there are no apparent grounds for holding that any strict analogy of proportion *in the sense in which Thomas earlier denies it*, or in any sense that does not presuppose analogy of proper proportionality, is countenanced by him.

Further, the virtual analogy of proportion contained in the analogy of effect to cause, and of one to another, can be shown necessarily to exclude what Thomas's teaching in *De veritate* insists must be excluded, namely, any determined relation of God to creature. Effect *qua* effect includes relation to cause, but in this case the divine cause does not of itself contain any determinate order to the effect, because nothing about the divine cause is of itself determinately ordered or has real relation to the creature. Normally a finite cause must undergo a shift from not causing to causing, and when that shift is undergone, it causes; but God undergoes no shift, is subject to no potency, is not in Himself really different after than before creation. Nor is God reciprocally limited in proportion to the creature as one finite cause limited by potency is limited by other beings: in relation to God the creature is *ab extra*, and the relation of God to the creature is conceptual inasmuch as God is not really ordered to the creature.

When in *Summa theologiae*, I, q. 13, art. 6, Thomas speaks of all analogy being of attribution ("Respondeo dicendum quod in omnibus nominibus quae de pluribus analogice dicuntur, necesse est quod omnia dicantur per respectum ad unum, et ideo illud unum oportet quod ponatur in definitione omnium"), it is reasonable to read him as referring to what he has commented immediately before in article 5, wherein he teaches that all predications analogously common to creature and God are such because of the causal relation. ("Non enim possumus nominare Deum nisi ex creaturis, ut supra dictum est. Et sic, quidquid dicitur de Deo et creaturis, dicitur secundum quod est aliquis ordo creaturae ad Deum, ut ad principium et causam, in qua praeexistunt excellenter omnes rerum perfectiones.") Of course, the effect *qua* effect is ordered to the cause, and so there is a virtual analogy of attribution. But (1) it is not extrinsic attribution (the creature truly is caused to be by God); and (2) it is not univocal but rather proportional by analogy of proportionality: *esse* is truly act in both creature and God, but in creature as proportional to the limit of potency, and in God as proportional to the full perfection of act unlimited by potency. The causality of God is ratified wholly in the effect, with no real relation of God to effect, whereas the effect is wholly ordered to God. Again, as *De veritate* indicates, this analogy of effect to cause, of one to another, can be only an analogy of transferred proportion, for the divine cause has no determined relation or proportion to the effect, although the effect is wholly determined in relation to the cause. As article 5 itself previously articulates it, perfections attributed to God signify God as incomprehending and as exceeded by God: and, one might add, as exceeded by God by no fixed proportion. Unless it is the case that in the span of one paragraph Thomas has literally forgotten this proposition, so that he thinks there is a determinate proportion and real relation of God to creature; or that he thinks the creature does not exist so that analogy of extrinsic attribution pertains; or else that perfections are univocally predicated of God and creature; then it must be his view that the proportion of one to another, and of effect to cause, are understood as analogies of transferred proportion that are always as it were convertible into analogy of proper proportionality.

While these teachings with respect to analogy of proportion may indeed be expounded and explained from the vantage point of the analogy of proper proportionality in accord with his earlier account, Thomas does not expressly reiterate his earlier arguments. But one must also add that neither does he deny them, and the very *ratio* at the heart of his point about proper proportionality with respect to God is contained in the proposition that perfections signify God such that they incomprehend God, and such that God exceeds them in perfection. The distance from the nickel to the dime is the same as that from the dime to the nickel, but there is no such determinate proportion between creature and God. Nothing in God renders God essentially to be creator: the relation is in God conceptual, whereas it is real in the creature. Had God not created, God would be identically the same.

Since Thomas neither expressly reiterates his earlier teaching nor denies it in his later work, the historical criticism of analogy of proper proportionality finally has little speculative weight. We must instead ask other questions: Did Thomas not anticipate that we would read his later utterances in conformity with his earlier ones—especially inasmuch as his earlier work articulates strategically central propositions he nowhere renounces? Did he not indeed write his later work in part precisely to address aspects of the relation of creature to God that he did not earlier treat? To use the phrase of Wittgenstein, one does not buy a second copy of the morning paper to confirm what the first one says: the fact that Thomas's later work does not dwell on his earlier affirmations is neither surprising nor sufficient to necessitate the judgment that he "abandoned" his earlier teaching.

Our view of the abandonment thesis may very rightly be a function of just how essential a teaching we take Thomas to have propounded in the analogy of proper proportionality. For example, virtually everyone takes the principle of noncontradiction to be essential to his work, and no one would dream of arguing that he abandons it because he later considers a variety of metaphysical issues without expressly reiterating it as a metaphysical principle. If analogy of proper proportionality actually and implicitly bears on the discovery that being is divided by potency and act, and renders being intrinsically analogous as designating a likeness of diverse *rationes* of act and potency; if indeed it is what makes the causal reasoning of the theistic proofs to be possible without equivocation; and if in *De veritate* Thomas defends an improper or extremely general or loose sense of analogy of proportion understood as presupposing analogy of proper proportionality; then Thomas's comparative silence on this point later in his career may be construed precisely as an indication that he has *not* changed his judgment on so central an issue.

As noted earlier,[7] Klubertanz considers the intrinsic role of potency in Thomas's doctrine of participation—which I argue to be an implication of the division of being by act and potency and to require the analogy of proper proportionality—to be a later judgment of Aquinas occurring subsequent to *De veritate* in his works *De potentia dei* and the *Summa contra gentiles*, thus marking a richer doctrine of participation. The role of potency in his earlier doctrine of participation is less clear,[8] but to the degree that this is ceded to be true (and "less clear" does not mean "not implicitly present"), it must be noted (1) that *De potentia dei* is still an early work, and (2) that the implicit enrichment of the doctrine of participation by the division of being by act and potency is both a clear implication of this division, and an implication properly articulable only through analogy of proper proportionality. For it is the analogy of proper proportionality according to which we contemplate the likeness of diverse *rationes* of act and potency, and it is these diverse *rationes* that mark out the differing degrees of participation. Simply and more strongly put: without the remotion of beings from the first cause owing to diverse *rationes* of act limited by potency, there is no Thomistic doctrine of participation. Even ceding the point about Thomas's own progression of insight from *De veritate* onward to *De potentia dei* and the *Summa contra gentiles*, there remains the datum that the doctrine of participation requires, for Thomas, the division of being by potency and act, and the analogy of being as the likeness of differing *rationes* of act and potency that demarcate diverse modes of participation of being through God's efficient causality. This fact makes the case all the stronger that Thomas did not simply abandon or renounce a doctrine so central to his teaching as the doctrine that being is analogous according to analogy of proper proportionality. The analogical formality of being is indeed prerequisite to the achievement of inquiry into efficient and final causality.

To illustrate the matter, consider the following computer analogy: what happens with Thomas's teaching is not like the fate of information in random access memory, which is gone from memory the moment that the screen changes; rather, it is like the screen saver, present and understood to be functioning even when not filling the screen. It is systematic analysis, and not merely the datum that Thomas does not reiterate his teaching, that must finally aid us in judging why it is that Thomas does not repeat himself.

After all, we have the perfect illustration of his own affirmation of the metaphysics of *esse* to instruct us that what he deems to be central and determining is not always bestowed a proportionate material place in his synthesis (but its formal role is beyond doubt). As is seen clearly in the *Summa theologiae*, Thomas often introduces his own metaphysics only after considering and ratifying various streams of the tradition as a whole and in their own right, showing at the end how his own development of metaphysics may aid in perfecting this tradition without unilateral stress on his own distinctive views. Despite its demonstrable centrality for his own theological contemplation, he is far from trumpeting the real distinction of essence and existence in all creatures on every page. We likewise see this tendency in his treatment of Augustine, toward whom Thomas shows such great theological regard that even where he disagrees with Augustine, he typically understates the actual differences. Given these proclivities, it is not at all unlikely that—just as Thomas's metaphysics of *esse*, developed in *De ente et essentia*, *De potentia dei*, and his *Scriptum super Sententiis*, are present but kept in the background of the *Summa theologiae*—so his doctrine of proper proportionality is kept even further in the background.

There is here a general question of how we should regard arguments Thomas makes in systematic works of philosophy and theology which are then either not mentioned or are understated in relation to the volume of material consideration in the text. One thinks, for example, of Thomas's decision in the *Summa theologiae* not to mention the *intellectus essentiae* argument for knowledge of the real distinction of essence and existence in material things. Some argue that this is an early treatment of Thomas, one influenced by Avicenna and then abandoned—but to the degree to which the argument can be defended on Thomistic grounds apart from the teaching of Avicenna, such a conclusion is hasty. It is impossible, then, to keep systematic judgment out of these considerations;[9] otherwise, the speculative importance of principles must be deemed equivalent to their mere textual proliferation, a judgment that would make the apogee of any philosophic doctrine to coincide with its syncategorematic terms. On its own terms, then, the historical objection is plainly insufficient to conclude the matter. This is all the more so if analogy of proportion, or of one to another, was envisioned by Thomas in his early work as possible solely on the model of proper proportionality, a view we will consider below when we treat the readings of Fr. Klubertantz and Fr. Wippel.

The "Two Thomisms, Two Analogies" of Montagnes

Bernard Montagnes has written a profound and influential study of analogy, *The Doctrine of the Analogy of Being according to Thomas Aquinas*,[10] that famously divides Thomistic understandings of being and analogy as between the formal on the one hand, and the causal or participatory on the other. Hence he divides the two accounts in the light of the following chart which he provides in note 1 of his conclusion (see Table 1).[11]

My objections to all the reticulations of his argument are too many to develop adequately without writing another work of equal length to this volume. Yet nonetheless, in principle it is possible to demarcate the precise points of difference in relation to the chart he provides. What is wrong with this division of the putatively diverse Thomisms of Cajetan vs. Montagnes' Aquinas?

First, induction either does or does not achieve an intelligible affirmation. If it does, then—since what it obtains leaves all

Table 1.   Montagnes' Two Thomisms

Formal abstraction or "intuition" of being	1	Separation or induction of being
Ens ut participium	2	*Ens ut nomen*
Limitation by composition	3	Limitation by formal hierarchy
The *perfectio essendi* identified with *esse*	4	The *perfectio essendi* includes essence, *esse*, and the subject
Metaphysics as theology	5	Metaphysics as ontology
Unity of the idea of being	6	Unity of the degrees of being
Analogy of proportion	7	Analogy of relation

subordinate actual formalities in the background—the result may analogically be designated as a formal abstraction or "intuition" precisely by means of judgment and implying a corresponding "idea." The insistence upon the opposition of "abstraction" to "separation" is true if abstraction is limited to the realm of apprehension; but in the *Summa theologiae*, Thomas clearly uses the terminology of *abstractio* to refer to judgment of separation.[12] One may cling to the hope that this is a manuscript error, but the simpler and more manifest answer is that the resolution to being achieved through the judgment of separation does indeed attain the formally analogical object of being: it does not attain nothing, nor does it focus on subordinate formalities. Hence it is altogether appropriate to refer to this as analogically an abstraction, which is precisely what Aquinas does.[13] Moreover, that there is an idea of being as intrinsically analogous according to the likeness of diverse *rationes* of act and potency is neither rationalist nor does it fall short of truth: being is intrinsically analogous according to the likeness of diverse *rationes* of act and potency. Often it is alleged that such an account would be indefensibly conceptualist given Thomas's emphasis upon the role of judgment in metaphysical knowledge. But this is not the case inasmuch as the positive judgment of *esse* is most formal, and the conception of being has reference to *esse* as proportioned to and activating diverse *potentia*, such that there is indeed a likeness of diverse *rationes* of act and potency. Nothing in this derogates the role of judgment or reduces existence to essence; but it does indicate that proceeding from and through judgments of being there derives a resultant and intrinsically analogical idea of being, an idea which always implicitly adverts to the inviscerated multiple acts of being in relation to finite essence as *potentia*.

One may similarly wonder why being as participated should be considered opposed to *ens ut nomen*, unless a nominalizing tendency foreign to the doctrine of Aquinas is imported into one's consideration. Being is not mere *flattus voci*.

Likewise, limitation by composition is, as it were, the interior seam of limitation by formal hierarchy. But formal hierarchy will never so much as be known save insofar as we implicitly and actually advert to diverse *rationes* of act and potency. Indeed, formal hierarchy *is defined* in relation to diverse *rationes* of act and potency. Of course, "limitation by composition" suggests that *esse* is finitized not simply by potency, but rather in relation to potency: i.e., God intends to create a being limited by potency and causes the proportionately limited act.[14] In any case, it is here that we see that without formal analogy, recourse to analogy in terms of participation and efficiency is impossible. But then, being is not merely a name. The relation of participation is of course consequent upon the creation and not prior to it, for the relation of participation is real in the creature but not in God—the constant teaching of Thomas. It is impossible, then, either epistemically or ontologically, to say that the relation of participation is prior to the composite nature of the creature, for the composite nature of the creature which is the effect of creation is presupposed by the relation of participation: if there is no created being, there is no relation of participation. Insofar as there is a created being, it is a composite of act and potency whose relation of participation is diversified hierarchically by the degree and kind of potency. Without the analogy of being as the division of being by potency and act, there is no relation of participation

(nor is the creature for Thomas Aquinas a "subsistent relation"—
language that he reserves entirely for the *sui generis* reality of the
Trinity).

In the light of this point regarding participation, Montagnes
argues earlier in the book that in creatures essence performs not
only a limiting function with respect to *esse* by receiving it, but a
positive function by specifying and determining it, and doubtless
this is true.[15] He also argues that in God essence is identified with
existence,[16] and of course this is unequivocally Thomas's teaching.
Indeed, while in creatures essence is both a formal measure of the
perfection of being and a limiting principle, it is in God the formal
measure of the full perfection of being. It is in the context of this
general discussion that Montagnes pens the following lines, which
appear to this author to be erroneous:

> One can recognize the perfection and the primacy of the act of
> being without undervaluing the essence, provided that one does
> not reduce essence to mere potency and limit, and does not make
> of it that by which beings are other than God.[17]

We could understand these words to indicate merely that created
esse is not first actually infinite and then somehow limited by potency, for created *esse* is caused by God proportionate to the nature
of the being created. But even so, it is the case that *esse* is limited in
relation to essence as potency. That is to say, act is not self-limiting,
but is limited only in relation to potency—finally, limited in function of the hypothetical but immutable divine intention to create
that which He creates, namely, some limited type of being whose
existence is caused by God as proportionate to its nature (which
last is to that existence as potency is to act). Montagnes of course
affirms this teaching in the immediate context of this discussion,
but in the passage above he is obviously reluctant to identify the
essence as potency as that in relation to which *esse* as act is limited.
This seems rather clearly to indicate that Montagnes' account fails
to see that what makes for the hierarchy of being is greater and
lesser remotion from the first principle owing to different degrees of

potency, and that what marks the creature is precisely the limitation of the perfection of act by potency. It is the truth that only God is pure act—*ipsum esse subsistens per se*—that distinguishes God from all creatures. Thus Montagnes argues:

> In sum, there are degrees of being because the perfection of being is measured by the essences according to their formal determination and limited by them according to their receptive capacity.[18]

But it is not formal causality as such that accounts for "degrees of being." Form, essence, and substance are said of God, yet God is not subject to "degrees." What is it in created being that constitutes the limit on its perfection of being? What accounts for the limitation and plurification and changeability of created being?

The answer is not: formal perfection *qua* specifying and determining (something true of the divine essence itself!). Rather, the answer is the fundamental truth that created essence is to *esse* as potency is to act. That is, when we ask formally for the cause of limit, manyness, and change, the answer is "potency," for to have a created essence is to have a potential principle vis-à-vis *esse*. It is, then, precisely because of potency that no creature has or can have unparticipated being or exist *a se*. This is indeed "that by which beings are other than God," and to forget this is to run the risk of losing our intellectual savor for the creature as such, and for the dialectic of act that requires resolution from various gradients of perfection to *actus purus*, that requires conclusion from moved movers to the unmoved mover, etc. Indeed, all actual formal perfection is inscribed within the superformal perfection of *esse*. Hence there can be no question of erroneously supposing that the perfection of created formal determination does not presuppose and absolutely imply its indigence with respect to act, nor likewise any question of denying the proportionate limitation of the creature's act of being in relation to its essential nature as potency.

As for identifying the *perfectio essendi* with *esse*, there is no denying that the *actus essendi* is *esse*; but acknowledging this does not require us to deny the transcendentality of essence or the perfection of the subject. Nonetheless, essence in creatures is not only a measure of perfection but also a limiting principle, and the subject is not identical with *esse*. This is the teaching of Aquinas *simpliciter*, and it is difficult to know what to say to the claim that essence, and the subject, are not in creatures both vis-à-vis the *actus essendi* precisely actualized, for denial of this teaching is the denial of Thomas's metaphysics of *esse*.

As for metaphysics as theology vs. metaphysics as ontology, insofar as metaphysics reaches to God as a principle of its subject matter, it very clearly reaches to a theological conclusion. But the subject matter of metaphysics is *ens commune*, and *ens commune* is an intrinsically analogical object embracing diverse *rationes* of act and potency, of existing and essence.

Opposing the unity of the idea of being to the unity of the degrees of being again fails to affirm that for "degrees of X" to have sense, X cannot be nothing. But nor can it be univocal. The unity of the degrees of being does indeed provide the unity of the idea of being, for both in reality and in intention being is diverse according to the diverse *rationes* of act and potency. But without the analogy of being understood in terms of diverse *rationes* of act and potency, degrees of being are unintelligible: the degrees are precisely in terms of diverse *rationes* of act and potency which yet are similar. How is this not analogy of proper proportionality?

As for analogy of proportion vs. analogy of relation, this framing of the matter is seriously confusing. According to Thomas there is no proper analogy of proportion, but only a transferred and improper analogy of proportion that must finally resolve to analogy of proper proportionality; and analogy of relation is simply another term for what Thomas calls an improper analogy of proportion (for owing to the divine simplicity, God has no determinate relation to the creature—there is nothing about the divine essence that requires God to be cause of the creature or that places God in any determined relation to the creature—whereas the creature has such a determinate relation to God).

Montagnes implies that analogy of proper proportionality is a merely logical affair. To the contrary, it is an *ontological* affair, for the unity of being is the analogical unity of diverse *rationes* of act and potency, a judgment necessary immediately after the principle of noncontradiction as a condition for setting aside Parmenidean monism. Montagnes seems to think that lacking any formally analogical sense of being, it is enough to speak of relation to the divine cause—which is completely to lose the very evidentiary basis of the *motio* toward God in causal reasoning, an evidentiary basis which is that of the ontological limitation of act in relation to potency. To quote Montagnes:

> The unity thus uncovered is perhaps less than that which the first theory proposes, but it is more rooted in reality and it does not rest merely upon the unity of our representation of being. To put it in a nut-shell, the metpahysics of the idea of being seems closer to rationalism and less concerned with judging the real import of our concepts than the metaphysics of the degrees of being. The theory of analogy, as we have observed, has shifted from metaphysics toward logic; there is no doubt about the significance of this slippage: a philosophy of concepts is substituted for a philosophy of reality. Such, it seems to us, is the most secret and most powerful inspiration of the two Thomist metaphysics that the analysis of the doctrines of analogy [has] enabled us to uncover. A veritable conversion to reality is required to rediscover the unity within beings, a unity which is an effect of that of their Principle. This is the price demanded for remaining faithful to Thomas's authentic thought.[19]

The present author shares with Montagnes the concern that analogy not be reduced merely to the plan of logic, nor to a philosophy of concepts substituted for a philosophy of reality. But it is precisely on this basis that the purely apophatic evacuation of the formal intelligibility of proportionate being should be resisted, for act and potency are not mere notions or concepts but rather realities, and realities in terms of which the primal analogicity of being is disclosed. It is true enough that the unity of proportionate being is an effect of its principle, but the principle is only reached on the basis of the reality of proportionate being, and the analogical unity characterizing proportionate being—the analogical unity of the likeness of diverse *rationes* of act and potency—is the evidence on the basis of which the principle is affirmed. Indeed, it is the teaching of Aquinas that the relation of createdness is *post factum* of the being of the creature: God precedes the creature absolutely as its cause, and the creature is wholly derived from the divine efficient causality, but what God causes is the being of the creature: nonexistent beings do not have real relations (although of course a real being is really distinct from a nonreal being with which it has only a conceptual relation). We see this teaching of Thomas everywhere, for he knows that while the *esse* of the creature is an effect of God, it is not itself a receptive principle but rather the act of being of the substance that grounds the relation of creature to God. One thinks of Thomas's *Scriptum super Sententiis*, lib. 2, d. 1, q. 1, which speaks of creation passively (for actively creation signifies merely the divine essence with a conceptual relation to the creature):

> If, however, it is taken passively, then it is a certain accident in the creature and it signifies a certain reality which is not in the category of being passive properly speaking, but is in the category of relation. Creation is a certain relation of having being from another following upon the divine operation. It is, thus, not inappropriate that it be in the created thing, which is brought into being through creation, as in a subject. In the same way, sonship is in Peter insofar as he receives human nature from his father, but [sonship] is not prior to Peter himself, but rather follows upon the action and motion which are prior. The relation of creation, however, does not follow upon motion, but only upon the divine action, which is prior to the creature.[20]

The relation of having being from another follows upon having being (to repeat: nonexistent beings do not have real relations and so the analogical formality of being is prior to analogy of relation or transferred proportion). It follows that the analogical formality of being is necessarily by nature prior to and indeed the condition of the relation of createdness, of the relation of efficient and final dependency, and so prior also to the analogy of effect to cause which is predicated upon it. God is prior to the creature, but the relation of createdness is posterior to the being of the creature. While it may sound attractive to say something like "the creature is constituted by its relation to God," this is, simply speaking, false: for it is not by the relation to God that the creature is constituted, it is by God that the creature is constituted, and following upon that constitution it is really related to God (but God is not really related to the creature, God is not essentially "cause" as though to be God necessitated creation). Since, in addition, the effect is *qua* effect always attributed to the cause, whereas the divine cause has no real determined relation to the created effect, there is manifestly no strong analogy of proportion between creature and God. Indeed, although the creature is really related to God as an effect, God is not really, but only conceptually, related to the creature as Creator. This causal reference to God as Creator and Lord is what Thomas refers to in *ST* I, q. 13, art. 7, as a "temporal predicate" that pertains only conceptually to God, and does so exclusively because of something that is true about the creature. Thus, the causal analogy which is the foundation of all analogous predication between God and creature is founded upon, and must be translatable back into, the analogical formality of being in terms of the likeness of diverse *rationes* of act. For no strict analogy of proportion is possible unless someone wishes to contradict Thomas in *ST*, I, q. 13, art. 5, by denying that the pure perfections affirmed of God signify God only as incomprehended, and as exceeding the signification of the name. It is, one recalls, because no determined relation of God to creature may be affirmed that only analogy of proportionality, and not of strict but only of "transferred proportion," is held by Thomas in *De veritate* to be reasonable.

It is precisely here—in superordinating relation to being and substance—that one sees Montagnes' position edging closest to that of authors who incline toward affirming that the language reserved solely for the Trinity be applied to the creature, i.e., that the creature be considered a "subsistent relation." Accordingly, evacuating the analogy of being by treating its internal differentiation through diverse *rationes* of act and potency as merely conceptual is a gigantic error. The created effects of the divine principle are effects at all only because they *are*; their differentiation in grades is a function of *how* they are—which, granted, is the effect of how they are caused to be. But we know the effect as a condition of knowing the cause, as likewise the being of the effect is what is required for the relation of being causally dependent actually to obtain *in rerum natura*.

One begins to suspect that because Cajetan contributes critically in certain respects to our awareness of analogy of proper proportionality, the latter is not uncommonly thought to fold wholly within his account such that if we vary from the latter even slightly, we must abandon this understanding of analogy. But the attention Cajetan pays to the semantic and logical aspects of this analogy does not suffice to reduce it to a purely semantic and logical reality, because the likeness of diverse *rationes* of act and potency is objective and ontological rather than merely semantic and conceptual.

It is being itself that is analogous, being itself that is divided by diverse *rationes* of act and potency.[21] And if we cannot know this with respect to *ens commune*, then there is no real evidentiary foundation for any causal ascent to God: that is to say, analogy of creature to God will become a fideist projection in the absence of any genuine foundation in created being for the causal ascent to God. That foundation is indeed a function of the limitation of created act in relation to *potentia*. Indeed, it is this that Thomas adverts to at the crucial moment in *De ente et essentia* when he must explain why, if there were a case wherein essence and existence were identical, there could be but one such case—an argument whereby he shows that *ergo* in every other case save one hypothetical instance, essence and existence are really distinct, even in separate substances.[22] To suggest that this is not the genuine teaching of Aquinas, or that he later abandons it, are both propositions lacking warrant in Thomas's actual teaching.

The claim that an abstraction by way of judgment of *separatio* cannot reach being as intrinsically analogous by reason of the likeness of diverse *rationes* of act and potency, is to claim that we cannot know the creature to exist: for *esse* is the alpha and omega of our knowledge. The claim that "the metaphysics of the idea of being seems closer to rationalism and less concerned with judging the real import of our concepts than the metaphysics of the degrees of being"—that it is rationalism to affirm that being is analogically divided by act and potency —needs to be countered by another claim. The counterclaim is this: to deny that we know being as intrinsically analogous by reason of the likeness of diverse *rationes* of act and potency is to deny the intelligibility of being *simpliciter*. It is a doctrine of the apophatic unknowability of proportionate being, such that the very intelligibility of cause and effect is lost, and any metaphysics of the degrees of being is rendered impossible. To say that X is less remote from God than Y and therefore is more perfect being, does not yet establish *in terms of what* X is less remote from God than Y. The idea of being is a function of judgment, judgment that affirms being in terms of the likeness of diverse *rationes* of act and potency. This is analogy of proper proportionality, and it is not merely nor primarily logical, but real. It is not merely the *idea* of being that is analogous, it is being. Thomists do not stop at the idea, but rather reach through it to that which is, and the idea of being as intrinsically analogous drawn from the likeness of diverse *rationes* of act and potency affirmed in judgment is one through which in judgment we rightly return to being. Conception and reason are not evils, nor are they tantamount to rationalism. Participation and causality are intelligible solely in relation to being; they are not a substitute for being.[23]

Two Critical Objections of Ralph McInerny

We follow the succinct response to Montagnes' global rejection of analogy of proper proportionality with an even more starkly limited treatment of two major objections forwarded by the renowned Thomist philosopher Ralph McInerny. In his book *Aquinas and Analogy*, he offers two strong central objections to the view that the analogy of proper proportionality is the primary sense of the analogy of being (and also, as he puts it, of "the analogy of 'being'"). Articulating these chief points of disagreement, he writes of Cajetan:

> Cajetan got Thomas wrong because he misread the text from the *Sentences* and because he tried to make Greek usage regulative of the Latin use of the loan word *analogia*. My first thesis is that Aristotle never used the Greek term *analogia* and its cognates to express what Thomas means by analogous names. Thus far, that is merely a terminological claim, not a claim that what Thomas calls analogous names and what Aristotle speaks of as things said in many ways amount to different doctrines. On the contrary, we have argued that they are the same.
>
> My second thesis is that Thomas never speaks of the causal dependence in a hierarchical descent of all things from God as analogy. That is, terminologically speaking, there is no analogy of being in Thomas. There is, of course, the analogy of "being." This is not to say that Thomas did not hold what others call the "analogy of being," but he could not have confused that with analogous naming.
>
> If he had employed this usage, he would have recognized that this was possible only by employing different meanings of the analogous term "analogy." He would not have confused the two meanings, pressing the real proportion or analogy of creature to God into analogous naming, as if it were a type of it . . . .[24]

With respect to the first observation, my earlier comment about Aristotle's *Metaphysics* IX, 6, seems directly pertinent, for that passage seems to this author a clear statement of analogy of proper proportionality as the foundational analogy of being. Thus there seems to be a very strong continuity between *De veritate* (and also the *Scriptum super Sententiis*) and Aristotle's *Metaphysics*, for as we have seen, Aristotle's language agrees unabashedly with what we now identify as the analogy of proper proportionality. To quote again part of that passage:

Our meaning can be seen in the particular cases by induction, and we must not seek a definition of everything but be content to grasp the analogy, that it is as that which is building is to that which is capable of building, and the waking to the sleeping, and that which is seeing to that which has its eyes shut but has sight, and that which has been shaped out of the matter to the matter, and that which has been wrought up to the unwrought. Let actuality be defined by one member of this antithesis, and the potential by the other. But all things are not said in the same sense to exist actually, but only by analogy—as A is in B or to B, C is in D or to D; for some are as movement to potency, and the others as substance to some sort of matter. (*Meta.* IX, 6, 1048a35–1048b9.)

The similitude of Aristotle's language with the language of *De veritate* is arresting. Having already spoken about the pertinent type of analogy as of the sort wherein "a thing is predicated analogously according to the second type of agreement, as when sight is predicated of bodily sight and of the intellect because understanding is in the mind as sight is in the eye," Thomas proceeds to state that "to this kind belong all attributes which include no defect nor depend on matter for their act of existence, for example, being, the good, and similar things."[25] This looks, to the unwary and perhaps overly delighted eye of one who rejoices in continuity between Aristotle and Aquinas (not something that anyone could usually blame Dr. McInerny for failing to exude), to constitute a strong continuity between Aristotle and Thomas, precisely on the matter of analogy. As Aristotle teaches in *Meta.* XI, 9, 1065b15–16: "Now since every kind of thing is divided into the potential and the real, I call the actualization of the potential as such, motion." At least in the case of being, the transcendentals and pure perfections, and act and potency, it seems to this author that Thomas did in *De veritate* take up Aristotle's usage of "analogy."

With respect to the second large criticism offered by McInerny, this present treatment shares a measure of concurrence: for it is no part of my thesis that the analogy of being can substitute for the causal reasoning whereby one moves from the being common to substance and the categories to the causal inference that God exists. Hence, at least part of what is signified by the following words seems to me to be true: "My second thesis is that Thomas never speaks of the causal dependence in a hierarchical descent of all things from God as analogy. That is, terminologically speaking, there is no analogy of being in St. Thomas." Or, to agree while yet disagreeing—because as said above with respect to the agreement of Thomas and Aristotle, it seems that there *is* an analogy of being as divided by act and potency—it is not that Thomas never speaks of causal dependence in hierarchic descent of all things from God as analogy, as, after all, the analogy of effect to cause arguably extends to this. Rather, it is that the analogy of effect to cause, and of one to another, is an improper and "transferred" analogy of proportion in the sense specified in *De veritate*, and consequently one which must finally be understood in terms of proper proportionality inasmuch as the perfection of God is quite literally boundless. Causality and participation presuppose the analogy of being in terms of the likeness of diverse *rationes* of act as more or less remote from the first cause. Hence McInerny's account seems rightfully suspicious of attempts to treat the analogy of being wholly in terms of efficiency and participation without any prior analogically formal consideration of the being common to substance and the categories.

Further, as we reason to God on the basis of being as divided by act and potency, we never directly cognize the unlimited supereminent perfections affirmed of God but simply affirm that these exist, and exist without limit of potency, as pure act (for act is not self-limiting). It is not as though we peer into the divine essence, there to *see* the perfections of which doubtless it is the case that it is truer to predicate these of God than of any creature (e.g., absolutely unlimited being, true, good, wisdom, love, mercy, justice). Rather, what we cognize are created perfections, and we infer that the unlimited act that is the cause of finite being must possess in infinitely supereminent mode all perfections lacking potency in their definition. But there is never any determined relation of God to created perfection, but only of created perfection to God.

Fundamentally, it seems to this author that under the sway of a preoccupation with the logical aspect of analogous predication, and by a type of accidental reduction of the metaphysical to the logical, McInerny's account momentarily occludes the presence in the texts of both Aristotle and Thomas of a real doctrine with respect to common being as divided by act and potency, and as expressable in terms of an analogical likeness of diverse *rationes* of act.[26]

That Cajetan's own account of analogy is so often taken to represent the triumph of the "notional," and articulated in terms of its virtues as a semantic and logical theory rather than as a genuinely metaphysical necessity, is perhaps one font of this difficulty. Perhaps another is the very formidable creative strength of Laval Thomism, and of Dr. McInerny in particular, in moving outward from the philosophy of nature to the inquiries of the positive sciences and to ethics and political theory,[27] whereas the judgment through which being is analogically abstracted involves a type of resolution distinct from that of other sciences.[28] As being is not discovered through any univocal perfect abstraction, but only through an "abstraction" by way of the negative judgment of *separatio*, it seems clear that for Thomas, from the beginning of metaphysical science, being is and can be, and so is and can be said, in many ways: i.e., it is intrinsically analogical.

The desire to vindicate the essential role of *natura* and of the philosophy of nature, and the rejection of overly fideistic accounts of the relation of philosophy to theology, aid considerably in explaining the concern that metaphysics not be conceived in an unscientific manner. Yet metaphysical science is such that its mode of procedure and even the discovery of its subject matter are quite distinct from the other sciences. I cannot take up this concern with the appropriate level of detail here, but the insistence upon the centrality of the philosophy of nature, and the importance of philosophy of nature in relation to the positive sciences, should not occlude the implicitly metaphysical character of many of the discoveries of philosophy of nature,[29] nor the distinct manner of its relation to metaphysics.

In sum, the emphasis on causal and participatory analogy that McInerny criticizes seems to ignore both the analogically formal ontological consideration of the being common to substance and the categories, and also the consequent semantic and logical formalities. By contrast, the view of analogy of being as merely analogy of "being"—as an exclusively logical doctrine—keeps a certain semantic and logical formality, but at the cost of losing the analogically formal ontological account of the being common to substance and the categories in terms of the likeness of diverse *rationes* of act and potency. And so, oddly enough, in response both to Montagnes, who wishes to propound a strong ontological account of analogy—but wholly as a function of causal participation—and to McInerny, for whom the doctrine of analogy is wholly logical, the answer is the same: that being is not merely a name, and so the analogical ontological formality of being is prior both to considerations of causal efficiency and participation on the one hand, and to logical and semantic categorizations on the other. Furthermore, it is prior not only epistemically, as that whereby efficiency and participation are known, but also ontologically, The analogical formality of being is prior ontologically because there is no participation until a composite being of act and potency *exists*. Thus only consequent upon creation of the composite being does there exist the participatory relation of creature to creator, for God has no real relation to the creature, but only the creature to God.[30] The effect of creation is created being, and it is consequent upon created being that the relation of participation obtains.[31] Participation is something real with respect to the creature, who is really related to God, but it is not something real in God. Of course, the persistence of Thomas in this teaching, in and of itself, makes it intrinsically unlikely that he should ever have come to suppose that any analogy of creature to creator could imply real determination of God in relation to the creature—which is the very reason why all analogical speech of God must finally translate into the language of proper proportionality, for there is no proper proportion of creature and God. God does not exceed the perfection of the creature by any finite degree, but rather without limit.

Indeed, Thomas's persuasion in *De veritate* with respect to this systematic analysis seems to the present author to underscore the necessity of the analogy of proper proportionality even for analogy of creature to God as effect to cause or one to another. This is so because (1) these necessarily fall short of strict proportion insofar as God is not really determined in relation to the creature, requiring recourse to proportionality; and (2) causal analogy metaphysically presupposes and sets forth from the analogical formality of being in terms of diverse *rationes* of act as limited by potency, just as the grades of being required for participation are defined by the diverse *rationes* of act, and as the relation of createdness, the relation of efficient and final dependence, can obtain only as consequent upon being. Likewise, the analogical ontological formality of being is prior to all logical and semantic issues whatsoever, inasmuch as (1) the first principle of logic derives from the metaphysical principle of noncontradiction and not the converse; and (2) the being common to substance and the categories is analogically divided by act and potency (at the highest level, being is divided by existence and essence). Precisely this is the reason for Thomas's famed utterance even with respect to predication that "all univocal predications are reduced to one first non-univocal analogical predication, which is being" (*ST*, I, q. 13, art. 5, ad 1).[32] For both being and "being" are analogous, and the second analogicity derives from the first.

Klubertanz's Systematic Objections

Of course, a completely thorough consideration of Thomas's remarks on analogy might reward attention by supplying the key to a consistent interpretation. We might attempt to consider every passage on analogy in every work that Thomas wrote. Klubertanz has of course famously undertaken such a task in *St. Thomas Aquinas on Analogy*, and he has strongly objected to the thesis that the analogy of being is that of proper proportionality. Accordingly, Klubertanz's systematic objections may perhaps be helpful in adjudicating the claims of analogy of proper proportionality as the analogy of being on which all metaphysical discourse is humanly founded.[33]

Klubertanz's objections are clear. Leaving aside the historical objection—which he shares to some degree inasmuch as he considers proper proportionality a straitjacket into which not every text of Thomas plausibly can fit—his principal objections to the view that the analogy of proper proportionality is the analogy of being are as follows. First, he considers proper proportionality to be wholly a logical doctrine focused on predication of terms. Hence he writes:

> To say, as the logic of the Cajetanist theory of proper proportionality requires, that neither the analogates nor any of their constituent factors are directly related, leads in the case of the analogy between God and creatures to an awkward dilemma. For example, either we know what wise predicated of God means independently of all reference to creatures, or we use the term neither from a direct knowledge of God nor by any reference to the wisdom of men. The first of these alternatives is ontologism, the second agnosticism.[34]

But of course, we know in one sense what "wise" predicated of God means—it means the perfection of wisdom with no limit of created potency—while in another sense we do not, because we do not directly *cognize* this perfection as identified with God in His infinite simplicity. That is to say that Klubertanz's objection will pertain to any Thomistic account of analogy between creatures and God because any such account must negate created limit of the perfections predicated of God while affirming that we have no direct cognition of such unlimited perfection, but rather are constrained to such predication on the basis of a causal analysis which sees that limited act can exist only as derivative from act that is not limited. In short, the analogy of being does not substitute for causal reasoning nor is it intended to do so; rather, it is the evidentiary foundation for causal reasoning. To criticize an account of analogy because this account will not do away with the need to negate the created mode of perfections as a condition for the predication of perfections of God is accordingly misguided.[35] And it is the causal dependence on God which is the basis for the likeness amidst greater unlikeness articulated in the analogy of proper proportionality. Existence is indeed perfection in God, and existence is perfection in creatures, but in creatures it is limited by *potentia* and in God it is not—surely a case of proper proportionality if ever there were one. Still, were it not ontologically a true perfection, existence could not be the source of a real though limited likeness of the creature to God—albeit a likeness exceeded by unlikeness; and if it did not exist first and without limit in God it could not be found admixed with the limit of potency in creatures.

What exists as one and undivided in God is in creatures multiple, divided, limited. Further, the datum that the creature is really dependent upon God does not mean that God is really dependent on the creature, and hence it is not the case that causal reasoning requires of us the denial of the ontological primacy of the analogy of proper proportionality. Nor is it a defect of that analogy that the reason for finite perfection betokening God is a function of its causal derivation from God, for this causal derivation is knowable only in relation to the analogy of being.[36] The causal account is engendered to begin with by the need, in the dialectic of act, to resolve act limited by potency into the prime cause and first act unlimited by any potency; thus it can hardly be held against analogy of proper proportionality that while divine perfection is not brought into a determinate relation to the creature, created perfection always and exclusively subsists solely within a determinate relation (of effect to cause) to God. As all likenesses of creature to God are surmounted by greater unlikeness, so the likeness of created to divine wisdom is surmounted by the infinite transcendence of the divine wisdom, for the divine wisdom is proportionate to God and human wisdom proportionate to the creature. Nor is this proportion merely "predicative," but also metaphysical (God *is* infinite; the creature *is* finite).[37] The efficient and final causal inquiry into being in fact achieves its aim and affirms as conclusion that the perfection of the being common to substance and the categories is derivative of the infinite divine perfection.

Yet Klubertanz proceeds to argue that proper proportionality is correctly understood as exclusively a doctrine of predication. As he puts it:

There does not seem to be any more than a verbal difference between what we have called predicational analysis and Cajetan's analysis of *rationes nominum*. If Cajetan had explicitly stated that he was doing only a predicational analysis and if his followers had so understood him, he would have made a clear contribution. Because his interest in analogy was mainly logical, his exposition is important for studies of the validity of reasoning employing analogous terms. Moreover, certain objections now urged in favor of agnosticism rest on the false assumption that all terms are univocal (or at best only secondarily analogous, to use a distinction to be made in the next section). Against this assumption Cajetan's analysis is entirely valid and useful even for our contemporaries. When interpreted as remaining on the level of predicational analysis, the work of Cajetan is, then, a real contribution to the theory of analogy, and entirely faithful to St. Thomas.

But Cajetan does not seem to have realized the relation between his own and St. Thomas's doctrine. Had he seen the multiple levels of the Thomistic approach, he would not have absorbed all the other analyses of St. Thomas into the one category of proportionality. In order to make such a reduction we must suppose that, when St. Thomas spoke of an analogy between God and creatures, he meant the same thing as if he had said "an analogy between our predication about God and our predication about creatures."[38]

Klubertanz closes by observing, "We shall, therefore, close this digression by reiterating, predicationally speaking, analogy is proportional predication."[39]

But just here is the difficulty. Analogy is only proportional predication because some subject is related to some perfection, a relation which in creatures is the real relation of potency to act, whereas in God there is no such distinction of potency and act inasmuch as God is the unlimited perfection of being subsisting through Himself. That is to say, that the predicational structure is neither merely predicational nor merely logical with respect to the being common to substance and the categories, but is rather founded upon the prior ontological structuring of proportionate being itself.[40] The being common to substance and the categories is a likeness of diverse *rationes* of potency and act. Surely the discovery of act, and of its relation to potency, has a priority in this story. But at every level of being, being is constituted in relation to act: in relation, first, to the *actus essendi*; then to essence and substantial form; and even to accidental forms and to the acts of operative potencies. Being is not simply predicated analogously, but *is* analogous: it is and can be, and is and can be said, in many ways. Unlike the being of God, the being common to substance and the categories can be added to, and this multipliability of being is a function of potency such that the division of being by potency and act yields different modalities of being which are similar (each *is*) and yet proportionally distinct (each is *differently*, neither the essence nor the act of being are simply the same). It is difficult to see why this point should be so difficult for contemporaries: it is not a point merely about the predication of being, but rather about proportionate being as constituted by one or more *rationes* of act and potency. It might seem that there would be one *ratio* if only one creature existed, and at that without accidents, because accident is a mode of being in relation to substance, and so there would be two or more modes of being. For there to be one *ratio* there would also be the need *not* to consider hypothetical being, a consideration that would suggest diverse *rationes* since we are speaking of one realization of a potentially pluriform being. Objectively the being common to substance and the categories must be analogical insofar as it is subject to plurification, for plural *rationes* obtain if several creatures exist or can exist. Additionally, affirmation of the one God Who supereminently contains the whole perfection of being without any limit of potency whatsoever clearly requires the likeness of diverse *rationes* of act implying no determined relation of God to creature. Klubertanz surely is correct that predicational analogy is analogy of proper proportionality, yet this is founded upon the analogy of being; for if, as *Summa theologiae*, I, q. 13, art. 5, ad 1, instructs us, "all univocal predications are reduced to one first non-univocal analogical predication, which is being," this is because the being common to substance and the categories is and can be in many ways. Predicative analogy reveals the antecedent metaphysical analogy of being.

Even to think of a possible creature is to hypothesize some *ratio* of act and potency. This is the evidentiary language of being. It would seem that only an overlooking of the metaphysics of *esse* (according to which every finite subject is to its *actus essendi* as potency to act), as well as an overlooking of the nature of the originative rejection of Parmenidean monism (achieved through the reconciliation of the metaphysical principle of noncontradiction with our intelligible perceptions that is made through the discovery of the division of being by act and potency), can account for the view that the analogy of proper proportionality—while right and proper with respect to predication—is not truly the analogy of being.

But it is being itself that is divided by act and potency, and accordingly the diverse relations of potency and act are the constitutive relations of proportionate being, and these are similar and yet distinct. Moreover, among the proportions of the analogical perfection of being is identity with the full perfection of esse limited by no potency whatsoever or to the least degree: in the case of pure act the proportion of limit to the perfection of act (which is self-evidently by its very nature not intrinsically self-limiting) descends to zero. Granted that in God there is no relation of potency to act, and thus merely a conceptual relation in God between, for example, essence and existence, nonetheless insofar as these designate perfections they genuinely pertain to God, as God is the full perfection of act and identical with this full perfection of act.[41] The foundation for reasoning to God is indeed proportionate being, which is shot through with real diversity of proportions of potency and act. These reasons thus frame the *sed contra* to the somewhat anomalous view that proper proportionality is only an account of analogical predication of terms rather than properly expressive of the analogy of proportionate being itself.

But Klubertanz has further objections. He considers the analogy of proper proportionality put forward in *De veritate* to be "obviously an extension of mathematical proportionality."[42] Of course, the introduction to analogy of proper proportionality is nearly always in terms of quantity. But the quantitative analogy is not properly analogous but univocal because in mathematical terms it resolves to one univocal term (2:4 as 4:8 resolves to one half). By contrast, Thomas moves to the proper case of analogy, e.g., his analogy of sight as predicated both of bodily sight and of intellection (which can also be expressed: light:eye as truth:mind). This is completely clear in *De veritate*, q. 23, art. 7, ad 9, where Thomas states that the analogy of creature to God is like that according to which we say that as the pilot is to his ship so is the ruler to the commonwealth, or "there is a likeness of the creature to God, because the creature stands to the things which are its own as God does to those which belong to Him." Klubertanz accepts this text as properly affirming the analogy of proper proportionality.[43] Surely, however, no one will suppose these examples to be "quantitative." Rather, the quantitative illustrations are introductory, intended to draw the mind, first to proportion in the mathematical sense before turning to proportion in the ontological sense of a likeness betwixt two differing proportions which likeness cannot be reduced to something ontologically univocal (man:*esse* as angel:*esse*, but man is not angel, nor is human existence angelic existence).

In the end, Klubertanz tends to depict as "Cajetanist" the view that analogy of proper proportionality has a central role in Thomas's teaching. Yet the texts indicating this role are written by Thomas, not Cajetan. As Klubertanz writes:

> But, a Cajetanist might object, all real analogy *is* proportionality. For St. Thomas clearly teaches—and it is quite evident—that different terms predicated of God are not mere synonyms; in the sentences "God is," "God is wise," and "God is good," "is," "wise," and "good" are quite distinct meanings or intelligibilities (*rationes*), distinct not only from one another but from their subject, God. Hence there are always four terms in every analogy, and the predicates are essentially proportioned to their subjects, not to each other. Wise as applied to God and wise as applied to Socrates are by no means proportioned to each other, and the meaning of one does not include a reference to the meaning of the other.

But it is not true to say that God and creatures are not directly related, for in the order of being the creature directly and immediately depends on God; and in the order of knowledge what we naturally know about God can never be completely disengaged from its origin in the experience of creatures. In like manner the predicates themselves which we use of God and creatures are related: in the order of knowledge any perfection predicated of God includes in its definition a reference to the creatures which have been experienced by us as possessing such a perfection. This inclusion of one analogate in the definition of the other is one of the points on which there is a chronological development in St. Thomas, as we have seen.[44]

Yet the insight that "in the order of being the creature directly and immediately depends on God" is causal, and a function not simply of the analogy of being, but of causal reasoning in relation to the analogy of being. Analogy does not replace causal inference.

The denial of determined relation of God to creature is not the denial of the determined relation of creature to God, precisely because as *De veritate* insists (q. 23, art. 7, ad 9), "there cannot be proportion between him and God in the proper sense of proportion as found among quantities" in which, as it were, the distance from nickel to dime is the same as that from dime to nickel. Hence as we have seen above, in *De veritate*, the very work in which Thomas argues strongly for the analogy of proper proportionality, he writes:

As Dionysius says, God can in no way be said to be similar to creatures, but creatures can in some sense be said to be similar to Him. For what is made in imitation of something, if it imitates it perfectly, can be said to be like it absolutely. But however the opposite is not true; because a man is not said to be similar to his image but the converse. But if the imitation is imperfect, then it is said to be both like and unlike that which it imitates: like insofar as it resembles it; unlike insofar as it falls short of a perfect representation. Thus it is for this reason that sacred scripture denies that creatures are similar to God in every way. It does sometimes grant

that creatures are like God and sometimes deny this. It concedes
the similarity when it says that man is made in the likeness of God,
but negates it when it is said in the Psalms, "O God Who is like
unto thee?" (*De veritate*, q. 2, art. 11, ad 1)

This is hardly the language of someone denying that the creature
depends directly upon God, but rather of one who denies that God
has any real relation to the creature such that God would not infinitely exceed, and be incomprehended by, any perfection derived
from creatures. Along these lines, Fr. Wippel, in his extremely
helpful work *The Metaphysical Thought of Thomas Aquinas*, writes
about this issue in relation to Thomas's argument in *De veritate*
q. 23, art. 7, ad 9:

> We should also note that in a somewhat later discussion in *De
> veritate*, q. 23, a. 7, ad 9, Thomas again appeals to proportionality
> as an alternative way of explaining the similarity or likeness be-
> tween a creature and God. Here Thomas wants to defend the point
> that man is conformed to God since he was made according to his
> image and likeness. Because of the infinite distance between man
> and God, there can be no mathematical proportion between the
> two in the way proportion is found between different quantities.
> But insofar as the name proportion is transferred to signify any
> relationship of one thing to another, there is nothing to prevent us
> from speaking of some proportion of man to God. Thus, insofar as
> man was created by God and is subject to him, man stands in some
> relationship to God. This first explanation on Thomas's part does
> not necessarily commit him to rejecting analogy of proportion and
> defending only proportionality.[45]

Clearly, if Thomas's later use of analogy of proportion can be separated wholly from analogy of proper proportionality in the earlier
texts, it will then be possible to suppose that Thomas dropped the
earlier teaching. Yet the passage to which Fr. Wippel refers clearly
means by "some proportion" precisely to designate analogy of proportionality, as the words themselves indicate:

Nevertheless, in the sense in which the term proportion is transferred to signify any relationship of one thing to another (*as we say that there is a likeness of proportions in this instance: the pilot is to his ship as the ruler to the commonwealth*), nothing prevents us saying that there is a proportion of man to God, since man stands in a certain relationship to Him inasmuch as he is made by God and subject to Him. [Emphasis mine.]

The term "proportion" is transferred to signify any relationship of one thing to another "as we say that there is a likeness of proportions *in this instance*: the pilot is to his ship as the ruler to the commonwealth" (my emphasis). That is, the sense in which analogy of one to another is feasible, is a sense that presupposes or even is basically equivalent with analogy of proper proportionality. Is it not possible that Thomas persists in holding this view, and takes it as simply manifest that all relation of creature to creator as one to another will require a mode of comparison susceptible both (1) of retaining the determined relation of creature to creator, while (2) not placing the creator in a determined relation to the creature? It certainly appears from *De veritate* that he unequivocally took analogy of proper proportionality to be such an analogy, and subsequently to permit analogy of one to another in the precise sense that he specified. This could explain why Thomas sees no necessity in reiterating a point already strategically made—for indeed, analogy of one to another, and a "transferred" analogy of proportion, are not ruled out but rather made possible by analogy of proper proportionality. Thomas's position in *De veritate* appears basically identical with the one he articulates in *De potentia dei*, q. 7, art. 10, ad 9:

> If by proportion is meant a definite excess, then there is no proportion in God to the creature. But if proportion stands for relation alone, then there is relation between the Creator and the creature: in the latter really, but not in the former.[46]

It is possible to read the different texts of *De veritate* as though the author were not aware that these constituted a unity and so felt free to contradict himself and alter his position from textual monad to textual monad. So read, one will separate the language of both *De veritate*, q. 23, art. 7, ad 9 (which denies quantitative proportion but admits real proportion of creature to God—in the sense of a "transferred" analogy of proportionality—but not of God to creature) and that of *De veritate*, q. 2, art. 11, ad 1, from the language both of the main body of q. 2, art. 11, and from q. 23, art. 7, ad 9's clear embrace of proper proportionality. But this reading falls short of the clear unity of the position articulated in the text: that there is not analogy of proportion in any quantitative sense, nor in any sense which would put God in a real relation to the creature. There is an analogy of proportion in the sense that the creature really is related to God (although he also notes the unlikeness of the creature to God), and this analogy is founded upon and presupposes analogy of proper proportionality, for as we have seen, Aquinas states:

> It is true that, because man is infinitely distant from God, there cannot be proportion between him and God in the proper sense of proportion as found among quantities, consisting of a certain measure of two quantities compared to each other. *Nevertheless, in the sense in which the term proportion is transferred to signify any relationship of one thing to another (as we say that there is a likeness of proportions in this instance: the pilot is to his ship as the ruler to the commonwealth), nothing prevents us saying that there is a proportion of man to God, since man stands in a certain relationship to Him inasmuch as he is made by God and subject to Him.* [Emphasis mine.]

Aquinas's phrase, "in the sense in which proportion is transferred to signify any relationship of one thing to another (as we say that there is a likeness of proportions in this instance: the pilot is to his ship as the ruler to the commonwealth)," indicates that proper proportionality is still in the background. In this light, when he continues, "or it could be said that although there cannot be between the finite and the infinite a proportion properly so called, still there can be proportionality which is the likeness of two proportions," one might think that he is making the same point for that case in which someone prefers not to use the term "proportion" in its improper sense and merely as extending to "any relationship of one thing to another." Thus viewed, the difference between the early and later work of Thomas on analogy is this: later on he is content to use an improper sense of "proportion," taking it for granted that his audience is aware that this is not quantitative and does not imply that God has real relation to creatures or can be really determined in relation to creatures, as well as taking for granted that both in *esse* and in intention, terms predicated of God and creatures are analogous: analogy of proper proportionality. Whereas Thomas first needed to establish the metaphysical foundation naturally presupposed to theological analogy, with this established as the foundational context, "proportion" of one to another is utterly feasible. This is the order followed both within *De veritate* itself—where first proper proportionality is affirmed and then there is consideration of the analogy of "transferred" proportion or of proportion improperly considered and as translatable back into the analogy of proportionality—and also the order in which the metaphysical considerations of *De veritate* stand to the theological causal analogy taken up in the *Summa theologiae*. Even so, he reminds his audience in *ST,* I, q. 13, art. 5, that perfections signify God as incomprehending God and as exceeded by God (and exceeded by no fixed quantum of perfection).

Accordingly, mere advertence to Thomas's later extensive development of analogy of proportion will not suffice to indicate whether he intends to drop what he strategically has affirmed in *De veritate*, namely that with respect to analogy of proper proportionality:

> . . . a term predicated of God and creature implies nothing in its principal meaning which would prevent our finding between a creature and God an agreement of the type described above. To this kind belong all attributes which include no defect nor depend on matter for their act of existence, for example, being, the good, and similar things.

Being, good, and the like, are said by Thomas to be predicated of creatures and of God by analogy of proper proportionality. Nor does this imply mere agnosis about divine perfections. The affirmation of God as pure act affirms the perfection without limitation of potency such that simultaneously we do not know it in this way—while we do realize that what is signified is nonetheless the absolute maximum of the perfection lacking all the limitations of potency which contract it in creatures. The analogy of proper proportionality is rooted in the fundamentality of the potency/act relation in proportionate being, a relation that even enters into our contemplation of God by way both of affirmation (it is truer to predicate pure perfections of God than of the creature) and negation (the perfection is possessed by God as identified with His infinitely simple being without the limit of potency and so exceeds our knowledge and indeed exceeds the whole order of proportionate being).

As for Klubertanz's proposition that "in the order of knowledge any perfection predicated of God includes in its definition a reference to the creatures which have been experienced by us as possessing such a perfection," this is doubtless epistemically true with respect to the origin of our knowledge, but it does not establish that the sense of the created analogate as created is rightly projected within the perfection as it is in God Who excels and absolutely transcends all potency and proportionate being as such (for God does not fall under proportionate being, but it falls under Him). Accordingly, Klubertanz's argument falls short of showing that there is determinate relation of God to creature, although it is no part of the analogy of proper proportionality to imply that the creature lacks determinate relation to God (in a nonquantitative and "transferred" sense). Moreover, the determinate relation of creature to God is such that man is both like, and even more, unlike, God: "Thus it is for this reason that sacred scripture denies that creatures are similar to God in every way."

It is precisely for these reasons that Thomas clearly teaches in *De veritate* that analogy of proportion exists as presupposing analogy of proportionality. He later emphasizes analogy of proportion (understanding by "proportion" the "transferred" signification of any relation of one to another, rather than proportion in the strict sense—thus thoroughly ruling out any determined relation of God to creature, and so requiring the analogy of proper proportionality at its font), but he nowhere expressly renounces his earlier teaching. It is accordingly fitting to consider whether it is necessary to hold that Thomas altered his position when everything that follows by way of "analogy of one to another" or "analogy of proportion" may be argued to presuppose prior analogy of proper proportionality. If an author holds clearly in earlier work that B is possible in the sense of A, and then later elsewhere principally stresses B while still clearly affirming elements of A, we may still think the author has not shifted his intention but merely fulfilled it. Rather than thinking that Aquinas quietly abandons the analogy of proper proportionality, we may think that he has shown its ineluctability so pronouncedly that he can quietly continue to articulate the limited senses in which analogy of proportion obtains without ever implying abandonment of his earlier position. This is all the more pertinent because the earlier position expressly justifies analogy of proportion on the supposition that it is transferred to the case of any relationship of one to another and implicitly always able to be translated back into analogy of proportionality: "as we say that there is a likeness of proportions in this instance: the pilot is to his ship as the ruler to the commonwealth." Just so and similarly, one does not always retranslate the solution to algebraic operations back into whole numbers and fractions rather than simple fractions, taking it for granted that this is understood by the serious mathematician. At the very least the careful reading of the teaching of *De veritate* regarding analogy suggests that an improper and transferred sense of the analogy of proportion is compatible with and presupposes the analogy of proper proportionality. If this is true, then there is no particular reason why dwelling upon such analogy of proportion should be considered either incompatible with, or to require further articulations of, the analogy of proper proportionality. The author neither can nor needs to say everything everywhere. The negations that persist alongside the "analogy of one to another" and of "cause to effect" are sufficient to indicate that these are not *in sensu stricto* analogies of proportion in any determinate quantitative sense. Perfections affirmed of God signify God only as *incomprehending* God and as *exceeded by* God: there is no determined relation of God to the creature but only of the creature to God. Only strict analogies of proportion in the very sense ruled out by Thomas's clear teaching from the *Summa theologiae*, q. 13, art. 5, would suffice to contradict analogy of proper proportionality and so indicate that Thomas no longer held his earlier teaching. It follows that the abandonment thesis is simply not supported by the requisite texts unless the operative premise is that mere nonrepetition of a strategic teaching is equivalent to its renunciation, a position that requires an argument beyond itself for which nothing seems availing.

If the analogy of proportionate being is chiefly the analogy of proper proportionality in terms of potency and act, then this analogy will necessarily enter into the analogy of creature to God, for it is on the foundation of the being of the creature that causal analysis rises to affirm the reality of God. Hence all further discourse of God must bear the signs of this origin in created being. Here indeed is sufficient reason why the analogical perfection must be affirmed in God as incomprehended by us and as exceeding our understanding (by no fixed *ratio* but infinitely exceeding . . .). Analogy of proper proportionality is fitted to express the variegated *rationes* of potency and act in the creature whereby the creature's determined relation to God is articulated, and which is the source both of its real likeness and real unlikeness to God; whereas, it is also fitted to affirm God as pure act with no limitation of potency whatsoever, and in Whom there is no real division between wisdom, justice, and mercy because what we mean by each of these (which are not synonyms) is nonetheless found in Him as identified with His infinite simplicity, which infinitely transcends proportionate being (with which it has no real relation). Insofar as the total perfection of being must, without any limit of potency, be affirmed of God—on the basis of causal reasoning from being limited by potency—it would seem that there is no escaping the analogy of being as analogy founded on diverse participations of *esse*, diverse *rationes* of act. The analogy of creature to God is the analogy of act limited by potency to absolutely transcendent act unlimited by any potency, "because the creature stands to the things which are its own as God does to those which belong to Him."

That more can be said about creature and God in terms of the analogy of effect to cause and of one to another is a function of causal reasoning from the evidence of a proportionate being that is intrinsically and most formally analogical by analogy of proper proportionality, and which must be translatable back into analogy of proper proportionality to avoid any suggestion that God is placed in a determinate relation to the creature. But the "translating back" does not deny what even in *De veritate* Thomas clearly affirms, namely that in the general sense of any relationship of one thing to another, and ruling out any real relation of God to creature or determination of God in relation to the creature, one may in this transferred sense affirm analogy of proportion as, as it were, virtually contained within analogy of proper proportionality. It is the causal realization that the creature is really determined in relation to God that founds the judgment that the perfections affirmed of the divine cause exceed—but by no "proper" or determinate proportion, but rather infinitely—the perfections affirmed of creatures. And this judgment presupposes the analogy of proper proportionality inasmuch as there is no determinate proportion of God to creature, such that there is only improperly speaking an analogy of proportion "because the creature stands to the things which are its own as God does to those which belong to Him." Yet the inquiry into the ultimate final and first efficient cause of the being common to substance and the categories does explain, by a virtual analogy of attribution which folds into analogy of proper proportionality (so as to fall neither into univocality nor into extrinsic attribution), how it is that being and other perfections can be analogically common to God and creatures.

Both transcendental perfections and pure perfections are intrinsically analogous, and so susceptible of being affirmed without any limit of potency. This is precisely because despite always being found with potency in creatures, these perfections do not require potency—as being does not mean in the least not-to-be, nor truth mean falsehood, nor good mean evil—while yet in creatures these are always found limited by potency. Although being is divided by act and potency, potency as such is not necessary to act, while without act there is no potency. Thus neither in existence nor in notion are perfections the same—nor are they even only determinately different—as between God and creatures. Even among creatures, they are different in existence and in notion (for each creature, not just in species, but *qua* singular entity, is a composite being—even the angels are composed of essence and act of being—whose relation of act to potency is its own). The analogy of proportionate being as the likeness of diverse *rationes* of act and potency provides the evidentiary foundation for causal reasoning to the affirmation of God; and the same analogy of proper proportionality safeguards the divine transcendence and simplicity from any temptation to suppose that divine perfection exceeds created perfection merely by some determinate proportion. For the sum total of created perfection is infinitely exceeded by the divine perfection. Nonetheless, "the creature stands to the things which are its own as God does to those which belong to Him." The wise governor of the ship is wise, albeit limitedly; the wise governor of all that exists, is wise perfectly and without limit; and neither in existence nor in notion are these two wisdoms the same, while yet there is a likeness of diverse proportions. The creature is really and determinately related and ordered to God, but there is no real and determined relation of God to the creature: as the Fourth Lateran Council still teaches us, there is no likeness of creature to Creator which is not exceeded by a greater unlikeness: "between the Creator and the creature so great a likeness cannot be noted without the necessity of noting a greater dissimilarity between them."[47]

The Analogy of Being and the Transcendence and Analogical Intelligibility of the Act of Faith

If the act of faith and that which is materially comprised in it is to be intelligible, then true affirmative propositions must be formable about God. Likewise, if these propositions are to be true of God, then they must signify God as incomprehended and as exceeding the very terms of the true propositions. Nowhere are these considerations so vital as in regard to the act of faith. In the act of faith we hold fast to God the First Truth, revealing and revealed. But this cannot be to reduce God to merely and reductively human categories, nor can it be wholly vacuous of intelligible content. It would seem, then, that if intelligible content is considered as reductively or purely human, such that nothing can be known or affirmed of God, then the act of faith will be at best a limit concept with regard to the world, and a limit concept that can never be proposed such that its essential conditions could be even knowably possible. In short, the putative unintelligibility of the very content and object of the act of faith will have placed man in a circumstance in which agnosticism presents itself as the final cause of wisdom.

The problem here is not merely that of the *praeambula fidei*, although it essentially involves the rationality of belief in God. Rather, the problem is the fundamental problem of Christian discourse about God. The *via negativa* cannot be the sum of the story because negations presuppose prior affirmations. If no true and nonreductive affirmations can be made about God—affirmations that do not reduce God to human categories and so constitute speech not about God but about a conceptual idol—then theism and the very idea of divine revelation become pure leaps of faith, utterly nonrational acts founded upon and foundable upon nothing that could even remotely justify them.[1]

It is precisely here that the measured distinctions of Aquinas regarding analogy—and especially those he offered early in his career that indicate why all analogy of proportion is only improperly and by transferrence so called—are necessary. It is true that there is no real proportion of God to man, because no finite determinate measure can be assigned to the excess of divine over created perfection. Yet there is a real proportion of creature to God such that the creature is an effect of God. God is the cause of finite being, although—unlike other causes—there is absolutely no necessity for this causation, because God is the end absolutely speaking and so is ordered necessarily to no end *ab extra*, including that of the being of creatures. That which accounts for causality—superabundance of being—by its absoluteness in this case also provides the reason why no causing need occur. (The cause is already infinitely complete without causing, and so any causing is purely adventitious and unnecessary to God.)

All the language of dependence of effect to cause, and of one to another, presupposes this real relation of the creature to God. Yet God is not really related to the creature: whether the creature exists or does not exist, nothing is altered in the supreme divine perfection. Hence the real relation of dependence of the creature upon

God falls short of any proper proportion because it places God in no similar real relation to the creature. How then are we to affirm God as cause without simultaneously implying that this causality is in some determinate proportion to the creature, save through the analogy of proper proportionality?

One can say that *esse:creature* as *esse*:God insofar as in each case *esse* is act, and in each case *esse* is act proportionate to the subject—proportionate to the finite subject contracted by potency, and proportionate to the infinite subject uncontracted by potency. But are we not now back to mere predication, about which—as Klubertanz admitted—it is always true to say that predicative analogy is analogy of proper proportionality? Granted that in God there is no real distinction between subject and *esse*, subject and *esse* are yet indeed rightly said of God, and God is both subject and *esse*, so that while the distinction betwixt them is merely conceptual, the absolute transcendence in pure perfection of God is not merely conceptual. And so the predicative dimension stands secondary to the real dimension, which is to say that the divine perfection infinitely overpasses any created likeness to it: hence it is truer to say that God *is* than that the creature *is*, and so likewise of any transcendental or pure perfection. Consequently, this is not merely a predicative analogy (as though what were being affirmed were not real perfections, thus erroneously confining predication solely to a separated semantic and logical realm). Rather it is one that makes clear that there is no determined proportion of God to the creature, that the transcendent perfection of God does not exceed the creature merely by some determined amount or degree.

Naturally *esse*—or any perfection affirmed of God—necessarily leaves God incomprehended by and exceeding our cognitive grasp: God does not excel the creature in perfection merely by some finite quantum or proportion. Analogy of proper proportionality—together with the limited, improper, and transferred sense of analogy of "proportion" in which we say that there is an analogy of any thing to any other thing, or of effect to cause, but which necessarily translates into analogy of proper proportionality—answers to the analogy of creature to God.

The real relation of dependence of creature upon God is first discerned in relation to the *analogia entis*, which is a function of the likeness of diverse *rationes* of act and potency in creatures: it is the analogicity of being and the limitation of act by potency that make possible and imply the causal resolution to pure act. In both the order of being and the order of knowing the analogical division of being by act and potency is prior to relation and causal participation: nonexistent beings participate in nothing, nor do nonexistent beings have causal relations. The analogical formality of being according to the likeness of diverse *rationes* of act is thus absolutely ontologically prior to causal relation and participation.

The analogy of being is also essential to our causal resolution to God because if being in the premises is not analogical but univocally material, then conclusion to an immaterial God would be impossible. The analogy of being implies the causal resolution to pure act because, as the logic of the fourth way most resolutely and metaphysically clarifies, diverse participations of formal perfection (which are diverse according to diverse *potentiae*) imply a maximum. Something does not come from nothing, and "nothing" is not a cause. Were a grade of being held to derive either from an equivalent grade of being or from an inferior grade, then no causal explanation whatsoever would be offered: indeed, inasmuch as the greater is caused by the lesser, then in some respect something is caused by nothing, which is hardly a causal explanation.

This profound doctrine of causal participation proceeds from the division of being by act and potency, whereby it is intelligible and which constitutes its evidentiary ground. Accordingly, it makes very little sense indeed to separate the analogicity of being as divided by act and potency from the consequent doctrine of participation for which the evidence is indeed precisely the analogicity of being. The doctrine of participation presupposes the division of being by act and potency. Without this division, there is no Thomistic doctrine of participation. Thus an account of analogy proceeding from causal hierarchy and participation cannot intelligibly be opposed to the analogy of being as the likeness of diverse *rationes* of act and potency, for it is only because of the prior division of being by act and potency that limit, multiplicity, and change accrue to, and yield diverse grades of, being. Indeed, without implicit reference to diverse *rationes* of act—diverse because of their diverse contractions to potency which thus indicate diverse degrees of remotion from the supereminent unbounded perfection of the first cause—there can be no knowledge of causal hierarchy and participation, and neither can these exist. (This is because the relation of participation, and of being an effect, is consequent upon the being of the creature as caused: the relation is real in the creature but not in God.)[2] For the creature really to be related to God, or really to participate the causal order, absolutely requires the ontologically prior being of the creature as the subjective ground of these relations. Nonexistent beings do not have real relations, and the real relation of createdness and of causal participation follow *pari passu* upon the being of the creature which is the divine effect. Q.E.D.

Of course, nothing in this derogates the benefit of the improper analogy of proportion of one to another, or of effect to cause; nor does anything about it render the doctrine of participation that flows from the causal analysis of the analogy of being any the less profound or important. However, the causal analysis that proceeds from the analogy of being, and the improper analogy of one to another and of effect to cause that therefore ensue, always presupposes and bears the formal limitations of the created being that constitutes the starting point of such knowledge. While the analogy of being does not substitute for causal analysis, the causal analysis moving to the affirmation of the truth that God is, and the corresponding doctrine of participation, always bear the marks of their origin in the contemplation of the being common to substance and the categories. Indeed, it is impossible to speak of efficiency and finality *sans* the formality, or indeed *super*formality, of being: and God never has a determined relation or proper proportion to the creature, which is why improper analogy of proportion must be translatable into analogy of proper proportionality.

Thus Thomas's doctrine of analogy safeguards both the transcendence of the act of faith—God is never reduced to any proportion to created being, true, and good—and the intelligibility of the act of faith. For while the created *modus significandi* of created perfections, the limitation of *potentia*, does not pertain to God, the *res significata* of these perfections—the very reality of the perfections as such—is more properly affirmed of God than of creatures. To affirm that God possesses without any limit of potency all transcendental and pure perfections, i.e., perfections whose nature does not necessitate potency, does not place any determinate limit on the divine excess or imply human comprehension of the same. Both in being and in intention or notion, perfections affirmed of God are thus different from those affirmed of creatures; yet there is proportionate identity sufficient for reasoning, and the intrinsic ground of the difference is clear—creatures are limited by *potentia*, whereas God is pure act.

Both the transcendence and the intelligibility of all speech regarding God are accordingly founded in the *analogia entis*. The analogy of being is the evidentiary foundation for the *praeambula fidei*, as well as the precondition for the terms of revelation signifying the inner life of God. God Himself must know the terms of revelation as such that their proportionate human intelligibility is susceptible of manifesting a distinct truth proportioned to God Himself: for example, that He is three in one; that there is generation and procession in God; that He Himself may be loved with the love of friendship; that His love is healing; and so on. Far from being opposed as idol is to assent to the true God, the analogy of being conditions from within our reception of natural and divine truth.

Not even fideists can avoid the necessity to explain how the language of revelation can signify anything to those who receive divine revelation. The analogy of proper proportionality safeguards transcendence and intelligibility both with respect to God as revealing—the first truth in Whom one's act of faith formally reposes—and with respect to God revealed through the doctrine of the Trinity, the doctrine of the Incarnation, etc. It safeguards transcendence because all that is said of God is proportioned to God as His own, without limit of potency and standing in no determinate relation to the creature; and it safeguards intelligibility because "the creature stands to the things which are its own as God does to those which belong to Him." The middle term is not a third thing under which both God and creature fall, but rather the proportionate identity of perfection limited by potency in creatures, with perfection in its utter fulness in God without limit of potency and as identified with the divine substance and first cause. If it is said that one does not directly know the divine perfection, this is true: the beatific vision is not a requirement for metaphysical causal inference.

We know God as unknown, and the divine perfections are always cognized by us only as incomprehending God (Who possesses every transcendental and pure perfection in one pure act) and as exceeded by God: this is precisely what the analogy of proper proportionality absolutely implies. This is the case for revealed truths, e.g., "begetting," "begotten," "one," "Son," "Word" and so on, because they are affirmed of God as exceeding any created limitation of perfection and as infinitely remote from the created cognate while yet proportionately identical with it. For example, in the trinitarian illustration of the psychological analogy, the sense of the divine Word as God's knowledge of Himself is infinitely different from, yet proportionately identical with, the sense of the human concept in man's knowledge of himself: the divine Word is identical with the subsisting divine nature, whereas the human "word" or concept is an accident distinct from man's substance. There is an infinite difference because in God all is identified with His simple and perfect act, whereas in the creature perfections are contracted to potency. This is similarly true of the analogy of love, which in God is subsistent—the love shared by Father and Son who is the Holy Spirit—but in human creatures is an accident. Thus we have infinite difference and yet proportionate identity.

Maritain speaks of the "superanalogy" of faith, and stresses well both the infinite difference between metaphysical knowledge and revelation—according as the first proceeds from created evidence and the second from God revealing—and the manner in which the intelligibility of revelation involves the divine choice of "the analogical signs of what is hidden in Him":

But a capital difference from metaphysical knowledge intervenes here. For in the metaphysical knowledge of God, it is from the heart of the intelligible that our intellect, having discovered the ananoetic value of being and of objects which belong to the transcendental order, rises, thanks to them, to the divine analogate. On the contrary, in the knowledge of faith it is from the very heart of the divine transintelligible, from the very heart of the deity that the whole process of knowledge starts out, in order to return thither. That is to say, from this source, through the free generosity of God, derives the choice of objects and of concepts in the intelligible universe which falls under our senses, which God alone knows to be analogical signs of what is hidden in Him, and of which He makes use in order to speak of Himself to us in our own language. *No man hath seen God at any time: the only begotten Son who is in the bosom of the Father, He hath declared Him.* If God Himself had not revealed it, never would we have known that the notions of generation and filiation, or the notion of three having the same nature, or the notion of being made flesh and of personal union with human nature, or the notion of participatibility in deity by the creature and the love of friendship with it, could be valid in the proper order of the deity itself, and in regard to the intimate life of God.[3]

Yet while God chooses objects that He knows to be analogical signs of what is hidden in Him (and one bears in mind that real perfections as participated by creatures are signs of God), the analogicity of these signs is along the lines of the analogy of proper proportionality: nature, person, generation, filiation, do not establish a determined relation of God to man. Without the foundation of the analogy of being, the "letters" of the divine speech would not exist, nor would the divine transcendence be retained in our affirmation of the superintelligible content of revelation. The analogy of being is necessarily presupposed by divine revelation, just as the existence of creatures is presupposed by their real relation to God (at this point it may be wearisome, but one says again: nonexistent beings do not have real relations).

To say that perfection exists in God with infinite supereminence and in its fullness, whereas it is found in creatures with the limits of finitude, is not to hypostasize perfection as a third reality transcending God and creature. This is so because there is no univocal sense of "perfection," nor any determined relation of divine to created perfection; yet we can say that God is infinitely more "being" than the creature, that God is infinitely more "wise" than the creature, and so on. Without analogy of proper proportionality, this would be impossible. Of course the sense of "exceed" is relative to what is "exceeded" even though it is not determinately relative in the sense of merely some finite quantum of perfection. Thus our knowledge of created perfection is the foundation for our contemplation of divine perfection even though the latter stands in no determinate real relation to the former. It is the causal motion from creatures to God as principle (which only proceeds from being as analogically divided by act and potency) that makes possible knowledge of God by way of excellence (wherein God infinitely exceeds in transcendental and pure perfections known first through creatures and with limit of potency, but not requiring such limit) and by the way of remotion (whereby all limit of potency is denied of God). Thus Thomas (*ST*, I, q. 13, art. 1, resp.): "Now it was shown above that in this life we cannot see the essence of God; but we know God from creatures as their principle, and also by way of excellence and remotion. In this way therefore He can be named by us from creatures, yet not so that the name which signifies Him expresses the divine essence in itself."[4] Thus also is shown not alone the foundational role of the *analogia entis* but of the *praeambula fidei*, since it is solely on the basis of the analogy of being as the likeness (a likeness that is not merely conceptual but founded on the real community of being) of diverse *rationes* of act and potency that causal reasoning is able to affirm God as principle of all creatures. Without insight into the analogy of being, the theologian will either erroneously suppose God to have a real determined relation to the creature—which negates the divine transcendence—or else will erroneously suppose that all perfections affirmed of God are merely metaphoric, denying the intelligibility, indeed the truth, of the act of faith. Transcendental and pure perfections, however, are more properly said of God than of creatures. The appreciation of *analogia entis* bestows to the theologian the savor of creation as the real subject of the causal participation signified by *exitus* and *reditus*. It thus is past time for a return of realist metaphysics to this teaching, which uniquely stands at the crossroads of Aristotelian and Thomistic philosophy and indeed is formally presupposed by all theological discourse.

Appendix

A (Very) Few Words Regarding Metaphysics,
Separatio, and *Abstractio*

It is not at all uncommon for "being" to be understood
simply as an empty logical genus. Thus, since outside of being there
is nothing, "being" is taken as a sort of extremely broad and univocal genus that is logically empty since when one subtracts what
is inessential to it one has subtracted all created finite things. Of
course, being is subject only to *imperfect* abstraction because unlike a genus the being common to substance and the categories
implicitly and actually contains all its inferiors. We have spoken
somewhat of this imperfect hold on being in our treatment of proportionate being as a *confusio*, an analogical likeness or ontological
fusing together of diverse *rationes* of act (diverse *rationes* owing to
potency).[1] As the frog is to its being, so the angel is to its; but the
frog is not the angel, nor is frog being angelic being. Such a cognitive apprehension of being is inferior in clarity and distinctness to

univocal and especially to quantitative knowledge, while nonetheless in its certitude it is superior inasmuch as all knowledge formally presupposes being.

Likewise it is not at all uncommon to find that being is construed not as logically empty, but rather as a whole that while still needing to be taken as a whole is taken to be merely material and aggregative rather than formal. Thus construed, the science of metaphysics could be practiced only by a mind that knew everything precisely as it is—as Aristotle puts it, a mind that commanded the sort of knowledge that God most of all could be expected to possess. On such a view, the best that metaphysics could be for the creature would be the most inclusive aggregative knowledge of the various compartments of human learning available at any moment. Thus construed, being is simply an ideal asymptotically approached by minds that seek to gain the totality of knowledge, but is not in any strict sense a proper object of a distinct science.

This second view is also false, or rather deceptively incomplete: for while being may indeed be taken materially, the being analogically common to substance and the categories is intelligible, and involves a certain necessary-whilst-analogical structure and principles. Hence cause, effect, substance, accident, act, potency, form, matter, end, supposit, and so on are all analogical principles. Indeed, the principles of identity and noncontradiction are properly analogical in scope: every being is what it is, and being is not nonbeing.

These reflections are not without immediate practical implication for intellectual life today, for many interdisciplinary programs or projects of study presuppose only an aggregative sense of the whole of being; consequently, the analogical presence of being, cause, effect, substance, accident, act, potency, form, matter, end, supposit, and so on, are lost to view, and the intelligible analogical structuring principles of being and knowledge are thus lost at the most foundationally comprehensive level.[2]

The issue of *separatio* and of *abstractio* thus arrives when we ask how is it that being most formally viewed is discovered as fitting subject matter for a distinctive science? Thomas's well-known answer in his *Commentary on Boethius's De trinitate* develops from his view, articulated in that work, that the intellectual act of judgment is distinctively ordered to *esse*.[3] Thomas argues that knowledge that one thing really may be or be understood apart from another is attained through a judgment of separation, as distinct from acts of *abstraction*, which occur through apprehension of some form that may be taken in apart from other principles with which it is nonetheless really found or upon which it really depends.

Thus, with respect to the discovery of being as the subject matter for a science, Thomas holds it to be attained through a judgment of separation wherein one judges that being can be and be known apart from matter and motion, and not merely in abstraction (which he treats in the *Commentary on Boethius's De trinitate* as purely a function of apprehension) whereby one merely considers one thing apart from another even though to be or to be known the one may yet require the other. Of course, Thomas famously distinguishes the *abstractio totius* whereby one considers the nature as a whole, which is characteristic of natural philosophy, from the *abstractio formae* whereby one attains some form (e.g., Thomas says, mathematical form), and from *separatio* whereby one knows objects that exist separate from matter and motion and thus are known apart from matter and motion.[4] For in the first operation (nature abstracted as a whole, e.g., "horse"), the object can neither be nor be known apart from matter and motion; whereas in the second the object cannot exist without matter and motion but can be known apart from matter (although not apart from intelligible matter) and motion (e.g., quantity); and with the third the object (being) needs matter and motion neither to be nor to be known.

This teaching is too well known among contemporary Thomists to require a great deal of summary, having been addressed formally by authors from Jacques Maritain to Fr. John Wippel.[5] There is of course a prominent debate over what the conditions are for the judgment of separation. Specifically, does the judgment of separation require positive demonstration of God or of the immortal spiritual soul? Or can it be known that being is separate from matter and motion because in its intrinsic analogicity being overpasses the whole line of material quiddity as such? I addressed this question earlier by pointing out that the irreducibility of being to any genus or species indicates that it overpasses the line of material essence, and that only the analogicity of being in the premises permits us to conclude arguments to the existence of God. (Thus, "is" cannot mean merely "is material," or else the "is" of the conclusion of the proofs will necessarily mean this, too, implying that God is material being, which is false.) The final reason for this is that act as such is not self-limiting, because being as such is not nonbeing and the limit upon being is always a function of its relation to potency. That being overpasses material essence by reason of *esse* thus indicates that potency and matter exist owing to *esse*, and not the converse, just as potency always exists for the sake of act and not the converse. The limitation of act in relation to potency does not conceal from the intellect that act is not a limiting principle.

What seems worthy of note here is twofold. First, what is attained in the judgment of separation is being as not requiring matter and motion either to be or be known. And although all lesser formalities are invoscerated within being, in judging that being does not require matter and motion one is not denying that such lesser formalities are, but rather one is not expressly focusing upon them even though they are contained within being.[6] This is in an obvious sense to abstract from them, not in the sense of separating them from being (although being as such is separable from them inasmuch as they can not-be), but in the sense that the discovery of being *qua* being as subject matter for a distinct science does not itself require the formal aspect, say, of "tree" or of "magnesium" or of "radiation." "Tree" and "magnesium" and "radiation" surely are, but considering them as such is different from considering them precisely *qua* being. Indeed, were there no trees, no magnesium, and no radiation, other beings would exist, while yet others could exist. And so in a sense the knowledge of being "abstracts" from lesser formalities without precluding them precisely because these lesser formalities may or may not be, and if they are they are not by virtue of *what* they are, but by virtue of actual existing. Being as "that which is" is intrinsically analogous, contains many different modes, and is susceptible of addition. Upon the demonstration of the existence of God, we become aware that this essential analogicity of the being common to substance and the categories is the created reflection of the truth that God is imitable in many ways.

Second, the datum that separation occurs by way of the judgment that being, substance, act, potency do not require matter to be or to be understood, seems to require already the judgment that act is not self-limiting—the very judgment, in a sense, that requires the discovery of *potentia* in order to reconcile the principle of noncontradiction as a principle of being with our experience of many, limited, changing beings. For what is "most formal" in being is *esse*—what is most formal in *that which is*, is the "is." Now, through the judgment of separation, we attain being as such and not merely in the limited sense of any particular one of its actual or possible limiting modes consequent upon potency: we attain that which is. Thus, we might well think that this is indeed a certain sort of abstraction in the general sense of considering things precisely under the aspect of being while not bringing into formal consideration all the lesser formalities really or possibly included within being (as tree, magnesium, and radiation are lesser formalities included within being). This is not to say that it is merely *esse* that is separated in the negative judgment (*separatio*) that being does not depend on matter and motion to be or to be understood. Rather, it is to say that *what accounts for the relative transcendence of *ens commune*—of the being common to substance and the categories—in its analogous overpassing of all the various limited modes of being no one of which exhausts or is identical with it, is the relative transcendence of *esse*.

Matter and motion pertain to the essential mode of being—they pertain to a thing owing to its material quiddity—but *esse* transcends material quiddity. Indeed, if *De ente et essentia* is ordered to any single conclusion, it appears to be the conclusion that although potency cannot be known without reference to its appropriate act, essence as *potentia* vis-à-vis *esse* is known as really distinct from and as ordered to its existence. But even before discovering the real distinction of essence and existence, it is clear that in overpassing its essential modes being cannot be limited to them.

There is nothing about being *as such* that requires being to be material, for materiality is an aspect of the mode or essence or given kind of being, and if being cannot be reduced to essential formality in any being it assuredly cannot be reduced to a principle of potency such as matter. If being is not an essential mode of being, it surely is not a mere part of an essential mode of being. Yet doubtless it is true that were God not to exist, there could be no metaphysical science precisely because the being common to substance and the categories objectively implies the existence of God: if A implies B, and not-B is specified, it implies not-A. The subject matter of metaphysics provides the foundations for objectively certain demonstrations of the existence of God. Thus there is a real sense in which, were it true that God did not exist, metaphysical science would not be possible—but this does not mean that one must be aware of this metaphysical entailment in order to apprehend the subject matter of metaphysics and begin to understand its principles. Thus likewise, there are remote entailments of mathematical principles which, were those entailments not to be valid, the principles would be impugned; but one need not in order to discover mathematics simultaneously intuit all mathematical implications.

Further, the judgment of separation whereby we realize that being can be and be known apart from matter and motion is the foundation for an intrinsically analogous concept of being drawn from the judgment that being is irreducible to any particular mode of being, including the quasi-genus of material being. Every negation presupposes some prior affirmation, and the affirmation upon which the negative judgment of separation is predicated is that of the analogicity of being as overflowing its limiting essential modes. As through judgment we pass to the reality, so the attainment of being as intrinsically analogous and irreducible to any species or genus forms our concept of being. For the concept of being adverts to the likenesses of diverse *rationes* of act known through judgment and in relation to potencies known through apprehension. Hence we conceive being as that which is, understanding that the "that which" as essential nature *exists*, that existence is known in judgment, and that the "that which" and the "existence" are and can be—and are and can be said—in many ways: i.e., they are intrinsi-cally analogous. We thus also enjoy a concept of existence as that which is the actuality of some capacity to be and which is known originatively in judgment.

Hence I believe that it is because of these considerations, as has been shown above in the text, that in the *Summa theologiae* Thomas uses the term "abstraction" in a twofold way. This "twofold abstrac-tion" is articulated in *ST*, I, q. 85, art. 1, ad 1:

> It should be said that abstraction may occur in two ways. First, by way of composition and division, and in this way we may under-stand that one thing does not exist in some other, or that it is separate from it. Secondly, by way of a simple and absolute con-sideration, and thus we understand one thing without considering another. Thus for the intellect to abstract one from another things that are not abstract in reality is not found in the first mode of abstraction without falsity. But in the second mode of abstraction, for the intellect to abstract things that are not in reality abstract one from another does not involve falsity, as is clear from the case of the senses.[7]

We can also cite Thomas from *ST*, I, q. 85, art. 1, ad 2:

> But some things can be abstracted even from common intelligi-ble matter, such as *being, unity, potency, act,* and the like, all of which can exist without matter, as can be verified in the case of immaterial substances. And because Plato failed to consider the twofold kind of abstraction, as above explained, he held that all those things which we have stated to be abstracted by the intellect, are abstract in reality.[8]

The abstraction "by way of composition and division" such that "in this way we may understand that one thing does not exist in some other, or that it is separate from it" seems to pertain to what Thomas speaks of as "separatio" in the *Commentary on Boethius's De trinitate*. And it would seem that it is through this type of abstraction that "some things can be abstracted even from common intelligible matter, such as being, unity, potency, act, and the like, all of which can exist without matter, as can be verified in the case of immaterial substances." Of course, the manifest sign of the truth that being, unity, and such principles can exist without matter is indeed the case of immaterial substances. But these latter could not be demonstrated if the being common to substance and the categories were not such as to afford the causal inference to such a conclusion. The analogicity of being in the premises is required if in the conclusion "being" is to refer to anything but univocally material being. Of course, the sense of being is enriched by the causal inference, because we then realize that the being of finite things is a gift, an effect of divine efficient causality and so participated being. If God did not exist, metaphysics could not be a science; but we may know that metaphysics is a science even before the demonstration of the truth that God is, because the premises that actually and implicitly contain and imply this conclusion are derived from being as analogically common to substance and the categories. As Thomas reminds us in his *Commentary on Boethius's De trinitate*, the subject matter of metaphysics is being, and God is reached only as a principle of this subject matter: it is in revealed theology that God in Himself is the principal subject.[9]

The reason for this emphasis upon *separatio* as equivalent to *abstraction by composition and division*, however, is to indicate that for Aquinas an abstraction by way of judgment is possible. And what follows from this abstraction is indeed an analogous concept of being, one which the mind passes through to being, and which depends upon both prior apprehension (we know essential natures) and upon composition and division (we judge these natures to be, and we see the analogical character of *that which is* as overpassing all the *differentiae* of being, which *differentiae* of course are a function of potency). Prior to the causal inference to God, it is not clear just how far the relative transcendence of analogical being with respect to matter extends. It is clear, however, that being is not merely material being, because matter is merely part of a formal part of being, a part of the essential mode, whereas being overpasses all its essential modes and is reducible to none. How, then, could it be a part of a part? It is likewise clear from the start that act is not self-limiting but is limited only by potency. Thus, being may be found with matter and motion, but need not be: nothing about "to be" implies either nonbeing or limit as such (the former ensuing upon matter and the latter upon the essential nature as potency in relation to existing); nothing about "to be" implies any contractive mode of "to be" whatsoever.

What is most formal in that which is, is the "is," such that being is a function of act itself, and it is this that renders possible the demonstration of the truth that God exists. Accordingly, the negative judgment of separation is reached—that being depends on matter neither to be, nor to be known (to the contrary: it is matter that depends on *esse* without which it will not be). In *De trinitate* Thomas distinguishes two ways of being separate from matter and motion, one pertaining to God and the separate substances that can in no way exist in matter, and the other to being, substance, act, potency, *et alia*, that may be found in matter but do not depend on it for their existence. As he puts it, after distinguishing the science that treats of divine things not as the subject of the science, but as the principles of the subject (philosophic theology) from the science that concerns divine things as the very subject of the science (revealed theology, the "theology taught in Sacred Scripture"[10]):

> But each considers beings separate from matter and motion, but in different ways, for something can exist separate from matter and motion in two ways. In one way, because by the very nature of the thing which is said to be separate it can in no way exist in matter and motion, as God and the Angels are said to be separate from matter and motion. In another way because it is not of its nature that it be in matter and motion, but can exist without matter and motion, although sometimes we find it with matter and motion. And thus being and substance and potency and act are separate from matter and motion, because according to *esse* they do not depend on matter and motion, as mathematicals depend on them which are not able to exist unless in matter although they are able

to be understood without sensible matter. Therefore philosophic theology treats separables in the second way as its subjects, whereas it treats separables in the first way as principles of its subject.[11]

Or, as Thomas puts it in the introduction to his *Commentary on the Metaphysics*:

> For not only are those things called separate in existence and thought that can never exist in matter, such as God and the intellectual substances, but also those that can be without matter, such as being-in-general. This however would not be possible *if they depended on matter for their existence* [according to *esse*; "si a materia secundum esse dependerent."] (Emphasis mine.)[12]

Likewise we find St. Thomas arguing in his *Commentary on Boethius's De trinitate*:

> We say that being and substance are separate from matter and motion not because it is their nature to exist without matter and motion, as it is of the nature of ass to be without reason, but because it is not of their nature to be in matter and motion, although sometimes they are in matter and motion, as animal abstracts from reason, although some animals may be rational.[13]

It is the overpassing of the entire genus of material quiddity by *esse* that renders possible this judgment that being is separable from matter and motion, for *esse* is most formal in being inasmuch as being is that-which-is taken under the ratio of existing. But that being may be subject to potency does not establish that it must be subject to potency, and there is nothing about "that-which-is taken under the ratio of existing" that simply in itself requires or necessitates potency.

It was indeed implicitly the principle that act is not self-limiting that constituted the foundation of the Parmenidean problem and required the reconciliation of the principle of noncontradiction with our direct experience of many, limited, changing beings.

Intelligence discerns that act is not non-act, and that any limit, fracturing into multiplicity, or change from act to non-act requires a principle diverse from act, namely *potentia*. It is unintelligible to affirm that that whereby a thing is is simultaneously that whereby it is not; the nature of any transcendental or pure perfection is not what accounts for any degree of the lack of these perfections. From the moment that the real principle of noncontradiction is understood metaphysically, it is evident that act is not self-limiting. Thus to address the conditions for *separatio* as though the Parmenidean problem had not already been addressed and rejected, and as though the principle of noncontradiction had not already been reconciled with our experience of the many, limited, changing beings through the discovery of potency and act as analogical principles really dividing being, is a significant disenfranchisement of the Thomistic intelligence from its rightful inheritance.

If we cannot know at the start by virtue of the principle of non-contradiction that *act is not self-limiting* (for act as such expresses no limit to the intelligence—which does not mean that we naturally intuit the beatific vision, but rather that we see that the limited act we know is such because limit accrues to it only in relation to the distinct principle of potency), then it is not "existential Thomists" who would have fallen prey to error regarding the conditions for metaphysics. Rather is it the case—if the principle that *act is not self-limiting* is not intelligibly evident by reason of the very analogical formality of act—that the whole structure of metaphysics according to Aristotle and Thomas would be incorrect. But it is not incorrect, because it is only by virtue of potency that manyness, limit, or change accrue to being.

Jacques Maritain of course reasoned similarly. Speaking of *De trinitate* he argued:

> This doctrine shows indeed that what properly pertains to the metaphysical concept of being is that it results from an abstraction (or a separation from matter) which takes place *secundum hanc secundam operationem intellectus*. ("Hac operatione intellectus vere abstrahere non potest, nisi ea quae sunt secundum rem separata.")

If it can be separated from matter by the operation of the (negative) judgment, the reason is that it is related in its content to the act of existing which is signified by the (positive) judgment and which over-passes the line of material essences—the connatural object of simple apprehension.[14]

Even should we at some juncture think that perhaps there may be only material things, we have before us the evidence whereby we may judge that that which is most formal in being is act and that it is only limited from without by a principle that is not non-being, and not mere possibility, but rather potency. Thus we may see that act precisely as such is not self-limiting. This is not of itself and immediately, absent our awareness of the different ways in which potency requires activation and activation ultimately requires pure act, tantamount to the conclusion that God exists. It does not mean that our intellect begins with infinite act. Rather, it means that act is known from the start as susceptible of grades only in relation to potency. We know this from the moment we grasp diverse *rationes* of act which as such are diverse because of diverse degrees and kinds of potency. This means that it is only potency that accounts for the limitation of act, such that it is hypothetically conceivable that there be the case of pure act. But Thomas does not reason in the fashion of Anselm: that it is possible that there be pure act does not suffice to indicate that this is the case, and so he unfolds the demonstrative inferences of the five ways and of the existential proof in *De ente et essentia*.

In realizing that being is irreducible to any contractive mode whatsoever, overpassing all such contractive modes, and in judging that being is not equivalent to "being material" because what is most formal in being is act and *act is not self-limiting*, we thus have the root justification of the negative judgment of separation. But this negative judgment of separation (that being as such, although it may sometimes be found with matter, depends on matter neither to be nor to be known, but *sans esse* matter is not) gives to the mind the positive and intrinsically analogous concept of being. And here too, Maritain's arguments, although they have been ignored, seem to this author to be fundamentally correct. Speaking again of St. Thomas's *Commentary on the De trinitate of Boethius* he writes:

> The fact that St. Thomas here employs the word *separatio* rather than the word *abstractio* (reserved for cases where the object separately grasped cannot exist separately) in no wise prevents this *separatio*—since it ends in an idea, and an idea the object signified by which is the farthest removed from matter—from being an abstraction in the general or rather proportional meaning of the word (but which is not produced in the line of simple apprehension of essences!). This "separation" *is* the analogical abstraction of being.[15]

Maritain continues:

> Between the *triplex distinctio* of the commentary on the *De Trinitate* of Boethius and the three degrees of abstraction of Cajetan and John of St. Thomas there is a difference of vocabulary, there is no difference of doctrine. The doctrine of the three degrees of abstraction has its basis in the *Metaphysics* of Aristotle, where it finds an equivalent formulation.[16]

Of course, it considerably clarifies matters that Aquinas himself in *ST*, I, q. 85, art. 1, ad 1 refers to a twofold abstraction, one by way of composition and division, and the other by way of absolute consideration; and that in ad 2 of the same question and article he uses the term "abstraction" with respect to being, unity, potency, and act: "But some things can be abstracted even from common intelligible matter, such as being, unity, potency, act . . ." What, then, is the ground for denying that an abstraction by way of a negative judgment of separation, and founded upon the aboriginal truth that act is not self-limiting and that act is most formal in being—a truth that is manifest in the transcendence and analogicity of being with respect to all of its modes or differentiae[17]—yields an intrinsically analogous concept of being? To be sure, the concept proceeds from and is the fruit of judgment, but it is precisely by virtue of this that the concept is adequated to the intrinsic analogicity of being.[18]

Further, while potency is essential to created being, it is not potency that makes a thing to be, but *act* in the existential order. It is not essential to "that which is" that the "that which" be *potentia* vis-à-vis "is"—howsoever much it is the case that this is true of finite things—for it is hypothetically possible that there be a case in which essence and existence are identical. And as Thomas argues very formally in *De ente et essentia*, (1) if there were such a being, there could *a fortiori* be only one, because *ex hypothesi* it would lack all potency whereby it would be plurifiable; and (2) it follows that in every other case with but one hypothetical exception, inclusive even of the case of separate substance of which we lack quidditative knowledge, essence and existence are really distinct. And because such being receives existence from without and is caused; and because there cannot be an infinite regress of essentially subordinated causes; therefore a resolution to the existence of God as pure act in Whom essence and existence are identical—*ipsum esse subsistens per se*—is necessary.

After reasoning to the truth of the proposition that God is, it is clear that this relative transcendence of proportionate being implies the reality of absolutely transcendent being. As the creature cannot crawl outside its own cognitive skin, this judgment must however be susceptible of being framed in the analogy of proper proportionality, i.e., in an analogy whereby perfection *sans* potency and so unlimited is not reduced to perfection as subject to potency and so limited—analogy that does not fall into the trap of implying that God exceeds the creature by merely some finite quantum of perfection, but which yet implicitly contains an improper and transferred analogy of one to another and of effect to cause. Such an analogy is the analogy of proper proportionality.

Thus we see that the following elements of Thomas's teaching are very closely conjoined:

(1) the principle of noncontradiction and the judgment that act is not self-limiting;
(2) the discovery that being is divided by act and potency;

(3) the objective truth that being is itself analogical with the analogy of proper proportionality according to diverse *rationes* of act (owing to diverse *potentiae*);

(4) the nature of the cognitive attainment of the former (being) as an abstraction occurring through the judgment of *separatio* and leading to the positive analogical concept of being *qua* being as intrinsically analogous;

(5) the safeguarding of the transcendence and intelligibility of natural knowledge of God, divine revelation, and the act of faith.

It is the Angelic Doctor who has shown us just how closely conjoined they are, through developing metaphysical science to the point of articulating the principles and analogical structure of being as such.

Notes

Latin texts for the works of Aquinas are from *Opera omnia S. Thomae*, one part of the online Corpus Thomisticum project of the University of Navarre. Available at http://www.corpusthomisticum.org/.

Introduction

1. This, one may suppose, is the upshot of the demurrers entered by Jean-Luc Marion (author of the continental tone poem to apophasis, *God Without Being*) in his essay "Saint Thomas d'Aquin et l'onto-théo-logie," *Revue thomiste* 95, no. 1 (1995): 31–66. There he mitigates and largely withdraws the application of his earlier remarks to the work of Aquinas. Yet the negation of Enlightenment reductionism implies some positive affirmative basis, whilst Marion, in company with an impressive host of contemporary commentators, is unable to supply any affirmative foundation for speech regarding God. This metaphysical vacuole, and the failure to begin to fathom analogy, thus persists in afflicting even those who wish to throw off univocal modes of speech that would place God in a determined relation to the creature and so deny divine transcendence. It is simply inescapable that this metaphysical lacuna should impede and obscure the intelligibility of the act of faith.

2. Joshua P. Hochschild has written a remarkable defense of the analogy of proper proportionality, chiefly in semantic terms: *The Semantics of Analogy: Rereading Cajetan's De Nominum Analogia* (Notre Dame, IN:

University of Notre Dame Press, 2010). But the very formal proposition that the analogy of being is indeed an analogy of proper proportionality—that being is not merely another place wherein a certain semantic theory flexes its muscles, but rather that even semantic theory is intelligible only because of the reality of the analogy of being—arguably requires an even more thoroughly metaphysical vantage point.

3. Fr. Robert Sokolowski, *The God of Faith and Reason: Foundations of Christian Theology*, 2nd ed. (Washington, DC: Catholic University of America Press, 1995). My appreciation is sincere for a systematic work of such penetrating insight that defends the divine simplicity and transcendence so powerfully and well. Such was also the thought of my old mentor, Fr. Jan Walgrave, OP, who reviewed Sokolowski's book in *Louvain Studies* 9, no. 3 (Spring, 1983): 319–21. He wrote: "From the first page one gets interested in this book and goes on reading it with undiminished satisfaction, for its unity of concept, its clarity, precise knowledge, and originality. It is an example of how classic Catholic theology should be presented to modern man in a fresh new way" (319–20). Yet he also wrote the following qualification, whose force seems to me undiminished despite the intervening years: "But he is rather sparing in regard to the *viae* of Aquinas. On this point, I must raise one serious question. In the second of his proofs, Thomas argues that there must exist a first cause that causes all effects and all their intermediate causes *sub ratione entis. Esse* is his proper and universal effect in things. Now, such a cause cannot but be the one *esse subsistens*, the creator of all things which are not their *esse*, but only receive it. The same is true of the assertion of God's existence as it results from the third, and certainly from the fourth, way. If this be so, it follows that the Christian setting, as defined by the author, can be established by pure philosophical reasoning and not only, as it indeed may be, by a mediation of the biblical narratives, culminating in the life and words of Christ. In the happening of the disclosure, the 'most fully . . . through belief in Christ' (p. 152) may be preserved yet with the addition 'but also through the use of reason.' Or would the author answer that the rational *viae* would be able to work convincingly when, and only when, the Christian setting is opened to us through belief in Christ. This would hardly convince me" (320–21).

4. E.g., *Scriptum super Sententiis*, II, dist. 1, q. 1, art. 2.

5. E.g., in *De sustantiis separatiis*, ed. H.-F. Dondaine, in the Leonine *Opera omnia*, vol. 40 [1969], p. D58. It is of course also noteworthy that although many contemporary interpreters insist that Aristotle had

no intention of affirming God as efficient cause of the cosmos, Aristotle's language in *Meta.* XII, 10, 1075a14–15, seems to suggest that God is efficient cause ("leader," i.e. one who directs and commands), and that as transcendent, "he does not depend on the order but it depends on him": "We must consider also in which of two ways the nature of the universe contains the good, and the highest good, whether as something separate and by itself, or as the order of the parts. Probably in both ways, as an army does; for its good is found both in its order and in its leader, and more in the latter; for he does not depend on the order but it depends on him." Aristotle, *Metaphysics*, trans. W. D. Ross (Adelaide, South Australia: ebooks@Adelaide, 2007). Available online at: http://etext.library .adelaide.edu.au/a/aristotle/metaphysics/index.html. For extended commentary on these questions see Enrico Berti, "Unmoved Mover(s) as Efficient Cause(s) in *Metaphysics* Λ 6," in *Aristotle's Metaphysics Lambda: Symposium Aristotelicum*, ed. Michael Frede and David Charles (New York: Oxford University Press, 2001), 181–206.

6. Throughout the pages that follow, this phrase—"likeness of diverse *rationes* of act and potency"—is used. Of course, the discerning reader will see that this is tantamount to "diverse *rationes* of act": but what makes for these diverse *rationes* of act is precisely the principle of potency. This intrinsic gradation of the perfection of act proportionate to the degree and kind of potency is indeed the foundation for analogy, and the evidential ground both for the doctrine of participaton and for the causal motion toward God. It is wholly unsurprising, therefore, that in this life our knowledge of God is never free of the epistemic signs of its formal origin in this analogy of the being common to substance and the categories.

7. This, of course, requires me also to engage a position equally skeptical of the effort to treat causal participation as the analogy of being, the analysis of Ralph McInerny to the effect that analogy is exclusively logical. I had the blessing of conversing with him about this before his illness, and communicated to him that his account was too important for me not to respond to it. While I do not concur with his analysis on this question, it seems to me to be vastly preferable to the emphasis upon ungrounded relation as the foundation for the analogy of being. Yet I do not believe the analogy of being is purely logical, because the analogical division of being by act and potency is real, and enters into the very formality of being.

8. James F. Anderson, *The Bond of Being* (New York: Herder, 1949).

9. John Knasas, *Being and Some Twentieth Century Thomists* (New York: Fordham University Press, 2003), 8 n. 12.

Chapter One. First Principles and the Challenge of Parmenidean Monism

1. Friedrich Nietzsche, *The Will to Power*, trans. Walter Kaufmann and R. J. Hollingdale (New York: Random House, 1967), 279.

2. Thomas would later argue that prior to creation there is only a pure possibility in relation to the divine active power. *ST*, I, q. 75, art. 6, ad 2: "As a thing can be created by reason, not of a passive potentiality, but only of the active potentiality of the Creator, Who can produce something out of nothing, so when we say that a thing can be reduced to nothing, we do not imply in the creature a potentiality to non-existence, but in the Creator the power of ceasing to sustain existence. But a thing is said to be corruptible because there is in it a potentiality to non-existence." ("Ad secundum dicendum quod, sicut posse creari dicitur aliquid non per potentiam passivam, sed solum per potentiam activam creantis, qui ex nihilo potest aliquid producere; ita cum dicitur aliquid vertibile in nihil, non importatur in creatura potentia ad non esse, sed in creatore potentia ad hoc quod esse non influat. Dicitur autem aliquid corruptibile per hoc, quod inest ei potentia ad non esse.")

3. Aristotle, *Metaphysics*, trans. W. D. Ross (Adelaide, South Australia: ebooks@Adelaide, 2007). Available online at: http://etext.library .adelaide.edu.au/a/aristotle/metaphysics/index.html.

4. Note here again: This is a likeness of diverse *rationes* of act, but what makes for "diverse *rationes*" is precisely potency; so to put the matter more expressly we may say "likeness of diverse *rationes* of act and potency," understanding that there could be no such diverse *rationes* of act save owing to, and in each case limited by and in proportion to, the principle of potency.

5. Text is based on the translation of H. Rackham, *Eudemian Ethics*, Aristotle in 23 Volumes, vol. 20 (Cambridge, MA: Harvard University Press, 1935, 1981). Available online at the Perseus Digital Library: http:// www.perseus.tufts.edu/cgi-bin/ptext?lookup=Aristot.+Eud.+Eth.+8.1248a.

6. In that text (*Meta.* XVII, 7, 1072b3–4) Aristotle teaches that "the final cause, then, produces motion as being loved, but all other things move by being moved." The point of this text is that God as ultimate

finality is not moved while moving, unlike other lower causes that presuppose prior motion—but this is not to deny that God is also efficient cause of motion: because the motion is *produced*. The evidence is formidable that Aristotle held a doctrine of what later comes to be called "physical premotion" within Christian theology and philosophy. As in the text we cited from the *Eudemian Ethics*, this teaching is a function of the division of being by potency and act, and of the analogous sense of the term "motion." It is unsurprising, then, that Aquinas, tutored by the metaphysics of act and potency, cites in *De malo*, q. 6, resp., the teaching of Aristotle as supporting evidence in respect to his own judgment regarding the divine motion of the soul. Of course, he notes that God moves the will as by its nature ordered indeterminately to many. Aquinas wishes to make clear that the divine motion is received by a power that is free because not merely ordained to one effect—he does not mean to suggest that as and when moved the effect is not determinate. A principle extending to diverse determinate effects does not cease to be free because moved from potency to act with respect to its own free self-determination; rather, its freedom is actualized by such motion.

7. *Meta.* II, 3, 998b22.

8. For example, in the *Sophistical Refutations* V, 167a2, and *Post. An.* I, 33, 89a23–24, Aristotle expressly teaches that to be this or that is not the same as simply to be. At *Post. An.* II, 1, 89b32–35: "e.g. if a centaur or a god is or is not (I mean if one is or not simpliciter and not if it is white or not). And knowing that it is, we seek what it is (e.g. What is a god? What is a man?)."

9. Of course, a genus is not predicated by priority and posteriority (the woodchuck is not an animal merely by virtue of its hierarchic relation to the great ape), whereas in *pros hen* analogy *being* is so predicated. But more properly, there is the analogy of being *among substances* to start out with, an analogy of proper proportionality.

10. Something that makes no sense because it denies that creatures properly have being—whereas it is *from* the being of creatures that the demonstrative movement to the affirmation of God sets out.

11. As note 8 above observes, there are indeed reasons to hold that Aristotle had at least a basic grasp of the truth of the real distinction of essence and existence. But quite apart from his textual evidence, and given that Artistotle does not develop this teaching extensively, what matters is that the doctrine of act and potency as really dividing being is the foundation of the real distinction of essence and existence as articulated by St. Thomas.

12. This does not suggest that act is not, in finite things, limited; rather, it means that act in creatures is limited in relation to potency. Of course, God intends to bring forth a being whose actuality is limited in certain ways—it is not that there is an undifferentiated univocal "pool" of act that is canalized into diverse *potentiae*, but that God in bringing forth creatures intends from the first that they have only a certain grade of actuality, and so the *actus essendi* bestowed by God to the creature is proportioned to and limited by its potency. But act as such does not denote limit, and limit comes to act by virtue of its relation to potency.

13. W. Norris Clarke, SJ, "The Limitation of Act by Potency in St. Thomas Aquinas: Aristotelianism or Neoplatonism?" and "The Meaning of Participation in St. Thomas," in *Explorations in Metaphysics* (Notre Dame, IN: University of Notre Dame Press, 1994).

14. Jude Chua Soo Meng, "Neo-platonic Infinity and Aristotelian Unity: A Critique of W. Norris Clarke SJ's Reconstruction of Aquinas' Metaphysical Development," *Quodlibet Journal* 3, no. 1 (Winter 2001), ISSN: 1526-6575. Available online at: http://www.Quodlibet.net.

15. For a profound consideration of this influence on Thomas's thought, see Fran O'Rouke, *Pseudo-Dionysius and the Metaphysics of Aquinas* (Notre Dame, IN: University of Notre Dame Press, 2005).

16. See George P. Klubertanz, SJ, *St. Thomas Aquinas on Analogy: A Textual Analysis and Systematic Synthesis* (Chicago: Loyola University Press, 1960), 27–29.

17. Klubertanz, *St. Thomas Aquinas on Analogy*, 28–29.

18. Klubertanz, *St. Thomas Aquinas on Analogy*, 29 n. 19.

19. Cf. the teaching of Aquinas in *De ente et essentia*, wherein the middle term in his argument for universalizing the real distinction of essence and existence even to the separate substances—of whom we have no quidditative knowledge—is the insight that all the ways in which plurification can accrue to being require *potentia* so that *if* there were a being in which essence and existence were one (whose essence were open to the full perfection of existence) there could be *only* one (for the hypothesis of pure act rules out *potentia* and hence manyness). It is from this foundation of the universal real distinction of essence and existence in all but one possible case—proved in an argument based on the division of being by potency and act—that Thomas proceeds immediately to demonstrate the existence of God. The Latin text and translation of this critical argument founded on the real distinction of potency and act is provided below in ch. 3, n. 22.

20. And indeed also to the question, "Why is the name of God properly *He Who Is?*"

21. It might be thought that surely the doctrine of the Trinity falsifies this proposition, for here is actual plurality of persons that is not in function of potentiality. But the Trinity is not "three Gods," but three Persons in one God, each of Whom is the one and the same God. Trinitarian ontology that loses sight of the real unicity of divine being, nature, and substance is implicitly liable to unfold a doctrine of polytheism that is contrary to the doctrine of the faith. The different relations of origin and procession within the One God do not yield many gods. The identical divine being, substance, and nature are affirmed of each Person of the Trinity, and so in a certain way there is not plurification of *being* in the Trinity because each Person is fully and truly the One God: the divine processions/relations exist in the identity of the same nature. Of course, this invitation to study the metaphysics of the Trinity unfolded by Thomas manifests not only how truly unique is the infinite perfection of God within Whom there exists perfect diffusion of life and love, but how the truth of metaphysics that being is of itself diffusive is safeguarded in the affirmation of the Trinity, showing that creation is not a necessary entailment nor God really related to the creature (although of course the creature is really related to God).

22. Jacques Maritain, *Existence and the Existent*, trans. Lewis Galantiere and Gerald B. Phelan, in Maritain, *Court Traité de l'Existence et de l'Existant* (New York: Pantheon Books, 1948), 147–49.

Chapter Two. St. Thomas on Analogia Entis *in the* Scriptum super Sententiis *and in* De Veritate

1. *Scriptum super Sententiis*, I, d. 19, q. 5, art. 2, ad 1: "Ad primum igitur dicendum, quod aliquid dicitur secundum analogiam tripliciter: vel secundum intentionem tantum, et non secundum esse; et hoc est quando una intentio refertur ad plura per prius et posterius, quae tamen non habet esse nisi in uno; sicut intentio sanitatis refertur ad animal, urinam et dietam diversimode, secundum prius et posterius; non tamen secundum diversum esse, quia esse sanitatis non est nisi in animali. Vel secundum esse et non secundum intentionem; et hoc contingit quando plura parificantur in intentione alicujus communis, sed illud commune non habet esse unius rationis in omnibus, sicut omnia corpora parificantur in

intentione corporeitatis. Unde logicus, qui considerat intentiones tantum, dicit, hoc nomen corpus de omnibus corporibus univoce praedicari: sed esse hujus naturae non est ejusdem rationis in corporibus corruptibilibus et incorruptibilibus. Unde quantum ad metaphysicum et naturalem, qui considerant res secundum suum esse, nec hoc nomen corpus, nec aliquid aliud dicitur univoce de corruptibilibus et incorruptibilibus, ut patet 10 Metaphys., ex philosopho et Commentatore. Vel secundum intentionem et secundum esse; et hoc est quando neque parificatur in intentione communi, neque in esse; sicut ens dicitur de substantia et accidente; et de talibus oportet quod natura communis habeat aliquod esse in unoquoque eorum de quibus dicitur, sed differens secundum rationem majoris vel minoris perfectionis. Et similiter dico, quod veritas et bonitas et omnia hujusmodi dicuntur analogice de Deo et creaturis. Unde oportet quod secundum suum esse omnia haec in Deo sint, et in creaturis secundum rationem majoris perfectionis et minoris; ex quo sequitur, cum non possint esse secundum unum esse utrobique, quod sint diversae veritates." I am happy to deploy here Fr. Lawrence Dewan's translation from his essay "St. Thomas and Analogy: The Logician and the Metaphysician," reprinted in his book *Form and Being: Studies in Thomistic Metaphysics* (Washington, DC: Catholic University of America Press, 2006), 87–88. I alter only one element, namely placing "measure" together with "intelligible character" with respect to the third type of analogy, because to my mind this brings out more strongly the aspect of ontological measure as the condition for intelligibility, rather than the reduction to the logical and semantic of which the analogy of proper proportionality so frequently is accused.

　　2. *De veritate*, q. 2, art. 11, resp.: "Dicendum, quod impossibile est dicere aliquid univoce praedicari de creatura et Deo. In omnibus enim univocis communis est ratio nominis utrique eorum de quibus nomen univoce praedicatur; et sic quantum ad illius nominis rationem univoca in aliquo aequalia sunt, quamvis secundum esse unum altero possit esse prius vel posterius, sicut in ratione numeri omnes numeri sunt aequales, quamvis secundum naturam rei unus altero naturaliter prior sit. Creatura autem quantumcumque imitetur Deum, non tamen potest pertingere ad hoc ut eadem ratione aliquid sibi conveniat qua convenit Deo: illa enim quae secundum eamdem rationem sunt in diversis, sunt eis communia secundum rationem substantiae sive quidditatis, sed sunt discreta secundum esse. Quidquid autem est in Deo, hoc est suum proprium esse; sicut enim essentia in eo est idem quod esse, ita scientia est idem quod esse scientem in eo; unde, cum esse quod est proprium unius rei non possit

alteri communicari, impossibile est ut creatura pertingat ad eamdem rationem habendi aliquid quod habet Deus, sicut impossibile est quod ad idem esse perveniat. Similiter etiam esset in nobis: si enim in Socrate non differret homo et hominem esse, impossibile esset quod homo univoce diceretur de eo et Platone, quibus est esse diversum; nec tamen potest dici quod omnino aequivoce praedicetur quidquid de Deo et creaturis dicitur, quia nisi esset aliqua convenientia creaturae ad Deum secundum rem, sua essentia non esset creaturarum similitudo; et ita cognoscendo suam essentiam non cognosceret creaturas. Similiter etiam nec nos ex rebus creatis in cognitionem Dei pervenire possemus; nec nominum quae creaturis aptantur, unum magis de eo dicendum esset quam aliud; quia in aequivocis non differt quodcumque nomen imponatur, ex quo nulla rei convenientia attenditur. Unde dicendum est, quod nec omnino univoce, nec pure aequivoce, nomen scientiae de scientia Dei et nostra praedicatur; sed secundum analogiam, quod nihil est dictu quam secundum proportionem. Convenientia autem secundum proportionem potest esse dupliciter: et secundum haec duo attenditur analogiae communitas. Est enim quaedam convenientia inter ipsa quorum est ad invicem proportio, eo quod habent determinatam distantiam vel aliam habitudinem ad invicem, sicut binarius cum unitate, eo quod est eius duplum; convenientia etiam quandoque attenditur non duorum ad invicem inter quae sit proportio sed magis duarum ad invicem proportionum, sicut senarius convenit cum quaternario ex hoc quod sicut senarius est duplum ternarii, ita quaternarius binarii. Prima ergo convenientia est proportionis, secunda autem proportionalitatis; unde et secundum modum primae convenientiae invenimus aliquid analogice dictum de duobus quorum unum ad alterum habitudinem habet; sicut ens dicitur de substantia et accidente ex habitudine quam accidens ad substantiam habet; et sanum dicitur de urina et animali, ex eo quod urina habet aliquam habitudinem ad sanitatem animalis. Quandoque vero dicitur aliquid analogice secundo modo convenientiae; sicut nomen visus dicitur de visu corporali et intellectu, eo quod sicut visus est in oculo, ita intellectus in mente. Quia ergo in his quae primo modo analogice dicuntur, oportet esse aliquam determinatam habitudinem inter ea quibus est aliquid per analogiam commune, impossibile est aliquid per hunc modum analogiae dici de Deo et creatura; quia nulla creatura habet talem habitudinem ad Deum per quam possit divina perfectio determinari. Sed in alio modo analogiae nulla determinata habitudo attenditur inter ea quibus est aliquid per analogiam commune; et ideo secundum illum modum nihil prohibet aliquod nomen analogice dici de Deo et creatura. Sed tamen hoc dupliciter contingit: quandoque enim illud nomen importat aliquid ex principali significato, in quo non potest attendi convenientia inter Deum et creaturam, etiam modo praedicto; sicut est in omnibus quae symbolice de Deo dicuntur, ut cum dicitur Deus leo, vel sol, vel aliquid huiusmodi, quia in horum definitione cadit materia, quae Deo attribui non potest. Quandoque vero nomen quod de Deo et creatura dicitur, nihil importat ex principali significato secundum quod non possit attendi praedictus convenientiae modus inter creaturam et Deum; sicut sunt omnia in quorum definitione non clauditur defectus, nec dependent a materia secundum esse, ut ens, bonum, et alia huiusmodi."

   3. *De veritate*, q. 23, art. 7, ad 9: "Ad primum igitur dicendum, quod sicut Dionysius dicit in IX cap. de divinis nominibus, Deus nullo modo creaturis similis dicendus est, sed creaturae possunt similes Deo dici aliquo modo. Quod enim ad imitationem alicuius fit, si perfecte illud imitetur, simpliciter potest ei simile dici; sed non e converso, quia homo non dicitur similis suae imagini, sed e converso: si autem imperfecte imitetur, tunc potest dici et simile et dissimile illud quod imitatur ei ad cuius imitationem fit: simile quidem, secundum hoc quod repraesentat; sed non simile, inquantum a perfecta repraesentatione deficit. Et ideo sacra Scriptura Deum creaturis esse similem omnibus modis negat, sed creaturam esse similem Deo quandoque quidem concedit, quandoque autem negat: concedit, cum dicit hominem ad similitudinem Dei factum; sed negat, cum dicit in Psal.: *Deus, quis similis erit tibi?*"

   4. *De veritate*, q. 23, art. 7, ad 9: "Ad nonum dicendum, quod homo conformatur Deo, cum sit ad imaginem et similitudinem Dei factus. Quamvis autem propter hoc quod a Deo in infinitum distat, non possit esse ipsius ad Deum proportio, secundum quod proportio proprie in quantitatibus invenitur, comprehendens duarum quantitatum ad invicem comparatarum certam mensuram; secundum tamen quod nomen proportionis translatum est ad quamlibet habitudinem significandam unius rei ad rem aliam, utpote cum dicimus hic esse proportionum similitudinem, sicut se habet princeps ad civitatem ita gubernator ad navim, nihil prohibet dicere aliquam proportionem hominis ad Deum, cum in aliqua habitudine ipsum ad se habeat, utpote ab eo effectus, et ei subiectus. Vel potest dici, quod finiti ad infinitum quamvis non possit esse proportio proprie accepta, tamen potest esse proportionalitas, quae est duarum proportionum similitudo: dicimus enim quatuor esse proportionata duobus, quia sunt eorum dupla; sex vero esse quatuor proportionabilia, quia sicut

se habeat sex ad tria, ita quatuor ad duo. Similiter finitum et infinitum, quamvis non possint esse proportionata, possunt tamen esse proportionabilia; quia sicut infinitum est aequale infinito, ita finitum finito. Et per hunc modum est similitudo inter creaturam et Deum, quia sicut se habet ad ea quae ei competunt, ita creatura ad sua propria."

5. And God is really identical with Himself even though the relation of self-identity is a being of reason as Thomas teaches in *De potentia dei*, q. 7, art. 11, ad 3–5; for the text, see ch. 3, n. 41, below.

6. *The Sources of Catholic Dogma*, trans. Roy J. Deferrario (St. Louis and London: Herder, 1957) [Original: Heinrich Denzinger, *Enchiridion Symbolorum*, 30th ed. (Freiburg: Herder, 1954)], #432, p. 171, the Constitutions of the Fourth Lateran Council, under point 2, "On the Error of Abbot Joachim": "But when Truth prays to the Father for His faithful saying: 'I will that they may be one in us, as we also are one' [John 17:22]: this word 'one' indeed is accepted for the faithful in such a way that a union of charity and grace is understood, for the divine Persons in such a way that a unity of identity and nature is considered, as elsewhere Truth says: 'Be . . . perfect, as also your heavenly Father is perfect' [Matt. 5:48], as if He said more clearly, 'Be perfect' in the perfection of grace 'as your heavenly Father is perfect' in the perfection of grace, that is, each in his own manner, because between the Creator and the creature so great a likeness cannot be noted without the necessity of noting a greater dissimilarity between them."

Chapter Three. Consideration of Objections to the View That the Analogia Entis *Is the Analogy of Proper Proportionality*

1. George P. Klubertanz, SJ, *St. Thomas Aquinas on Analogy: A Textual Analysis and Systematic Synthesis* (Chicago: Loyola University Press, 1960), hereinafter cited as *STAA*.

2. *STAA*, 27.

3. *STAA*, 94.

4. Later I will suggest that the use of analogy of proportion by Aquinas is precisely envisaged in *De veritate* as founded upon analogy of proper proportionality. Hence advertence to Thomas's later use of analogy of proportion, which Thomas in *De veritate* says is feasible insofar as the creature does have a determined relation to the Creator but not vice versa, and which he expressly indicates is to be understood on the model

of analogy of proper proportionality, does not suffice to indicate the abandonment of the analogy of proper proportionality.

5. *ST*, I, q. 13, art. 9, ad 3: "Ad tertium dicendum quod haec nomina bonus, sapiens, et similia, imposita quidem sunt a perfectionibus procedentibus a Deo in creaturas, non tamen sunt imposita ad significandum divinam naturam, sed ad significandum ipsas perfectiones absolute. Et ideo etiam secundum rei veritatem sunt communicabilia multis. Sed hoc nomen Deus impositum est ab operatione propria Deo, quam experimur continue, ad significandum divinam naturam."

6. *ST*, I, q. 13, art. 5, resp.: "Respondeo dicendum quod impossibile est aliquid praedicari de Deo et creaturis univoce. Quia omnis effectus non adaequans virtutem causae agentis, recipit similitudinem agentis non secundum eandem rationem, sed deficienter, ita ut quod divisim et multipliciter est in effectibus, in causa est simpliciter et eodem modo; sicut sol secundum unam virtutem, multiformes et varias formas in istis inferioribus producit. Eodem modo, ut supra dictum est, omnes rerum perfectiones, quae sunt in rebus creatis divisim et multipliciter, in Deo praeexistunt unite. Sic igitur, cum aliquod nomen ad perfectionem pertinens de creatura dicitur, significat illam perfectionem ut distinctam secundum rationem definitionis ab aliis, puta cum hoc nomen sapiens de homine dicitur, significamus aliquam perfectionem distinctam ab essentia hominis, et a potentia et ab esse ipsius, et ab omnibus huiusmodi. Sed cum hoc nomen de Deo dicimus, non intendimus significare aliquid distinctum ab essentia vel potentia vel esse ipsius. Et sic, cum hoc nomen sapiens de homine dicitur, quodammodo circumscribit et comprehendit rem significatam, non autem cum dicitur de Deo, sed relinquit rem significatam ut incomprehensam, et excedentem nominis significationem. Unde patet quod non secundum eandem rationem hoc nomen sapiens de Deo et de homine dicitur. Et eadem ratio est de aliis. Unde nullum nomen univoce de Deo et creaturis praedicatur. Sed nec etiam pure aequivoce, ut aliqui dixerunt. Quia secundum hoc, ex creaturis nihil posset cognosci de Deo, nec demonstrari; sed semper incideret fallacia aequivocationis. Et hoc est tam contra philosophos, qui multa demonstrative de Deo probant, quam etiam contra apostolum dicentem, Rom. I, *invisibilia Dei per ea quae facta sunt, intellecta, conspiciuntur*. Dicendum est igitur quod huiusmodi nomina dicuntur de Deo et creaturis secundum analogiam, idest proportionem. Quod quidem dupliciter contingit in nominibus, vel quia multa habent proportionem ad unum, sicut sanum dicitur de medicina et urina, inquantum utrumque habet ordinem et proportionem ad

sanitatem animalis, cuius hoc quidem signum est, illud vero causa; vel ex eo quod unum habet proportionem ad alterum, sicut sanum dicitur de medicina et animali, inquantum medicina est causa sanitatis quae est in animali. Et hoc modo aliqua dicuntur de Deo et creaturis analogice, et non aequivoce pure, neque univoce. Non enim possumus nominare Deum nisi ex creaturis, ut supra dictum est. Et sic, quidquid dicitur de Deo et creaturis, dicitur secundum quod est aliquis ordo creaturae ad Deum, ut ad principium et causam, in qua praeexistunt excellenter omnes rerum perfectiones. Et iste modus communitatis medius est inter puram aequivocationem et simplicem univocationem. Neque enim in his quae analogice dicuntur, est una ratio, sicut est in univocis; nec totaliter diversa, sicut in aequivocis; sed nomen quod sic multipliciter dicitur, significat diversas proportiones ad aliquid unum; sicut sanum, de urina dictum, significat signum sanitatis animalis, de medicina vero dictum, significat causam eiusdem sanitatis."

7. See the text at ch. 1, nn. 16 and 17, above.

8. *STAA*, 27–29.

9. For a masterfully brilliant speculative treatment of the nature and significance of analogy of proper proportionality, see Yves Simon's essay "On Order in Analogical Sets," in *The Philosopher at Work*, ed. Anthony Simon (New York: Roman & Littlefield, 1999).

10. Bernard Montagnes, *The Doctrine of the Analogy of Being according to Thomas Aquinas*, trans. E. M. Macierowski, ed. Andrew Tallon (Milwaukee: Marquette University Press, 2004), hereinafter cited as *DAB*.

11. *DAB*, 162 n. 1.

12. *ST*, I, q. 85, art. 1, ad 2: "But some things can be abstracted even from common intelligible matter, such as *being, unity, potency, act*, and the like, all of which can exist without matter, as can be verified in the case of immaterial substances. And because Plato failed to consider the twofold kind of abstraction, as above explained, he held that all those things which we have stated to be abstracted by the intellect, are abstract in reality." ("Possunt tamen considerari sine hac vel illa substantia; quod est eas abstrahi a materia intelligibili individuali. Quaedam vero sunt quae possunt abstrahi etiam a materia intelligibili communi, sicut ens, unum, potentia et actus, et alia huiusmodi, quae etiam esse possunt absque omni materia, ut patet in substantiis immaterialibus. Et quia Plato non consideravit quod dictum est de duplici modo abstractionis, omnia quae diximus abstrahi per intellectum, posuit abstracta esse secundum rem.") The "twofold abstraction" mentioned is articulated in *ST*, I, q. 85, art. 1, ad 1:

"It should be said that abstraction may occur in two ways. First, by way of composition and division, and in this way we may understand that one thing does not exist in some other, or that it is separate from it. Secondly, by way of a simple and absolute consideration, and thus we understand one thing without considering another. Thus for the intellect to abstract one from another things that are not abstract in reality is not found in the first mode of abstraction without falsity. But in the second mode of abstraction, for the intellect to abstract things that are not in reality abstract one from another does not involve falsity, as is clear from the case of the senses." ("Ad primum ergo dicendum quod abstrahere contingit dupliciter. Uno modo, per modum compositionis et divisionis; sicut cum intelligimus aliquid non esse in alio, vel esse separatum ab eo. Alio modo, per modum simplicis et absolutae considerationis; sicut cum intelligimus unum, nihil considerando de alio. Abstrahere igitur per intellectum ea quae secundum rem non sunt abstracta, secundum primum modum abstrahendi, non est absque falsitate. Sed secundo modo abstrahere per intellectum quae non sunt abstracta secundum rem, non habet falsitatem; ut in sensibilibus manifeste apparet.")

13. *ST*, I, q. 85, art. 1, ad 2. On this matter, Jacques Maritain in *Existence and the Existent* retains the language—and, arguably, the substance—of Thomas's teaching. Why, after all, should an analogical abstraction not be possible precisely through the judgment of *separatio*, and why should one suppose that the consequent concept of being is not adequated or that it is false?

14. On this point see the excellent and profound work of Kevin White, "Individuation in Aquinas's *Super Boetium de Trinitate*, Q.4," *American Catholic Philosophical Quarterly* 69 (1995): 543–96.

15. *DAB*, 88.

16. *DAB*, 88.

17. *DAB*, 88.

18. *DAB*, 88.

19. *DAB*, 162.

20. I was first struck by this passage in the translation offered by Steven E. Baldner and William E. Carroll, *Aquinas on Creation* (Toronto: Pontifical Institute of Medieval Studies, 1997), 77, which I use above. Cf. the Latin: *Super Sent.*, lib. 2, d. 1, q. 1, art. 2, ad 4: "Si autem sumatur passive, sic est quoddam accidens in creatura, et sic significat quamdam rem, non quae sit in praedicamento passionis, proprie loquendo, sed quae est in genere relationis, et est quaedam habitudo habentis esse ab alio

consequens operationem divinam: et sic non est inconveniens quod sit in ipso creato quod educitur per creationem, sicut in subjecto; sicut filiatio in Petro, inquantum recipit naturam humanam a patre suo, non est prior ipso Petro; sed sequitur actionem et motum, quae sunt priora. Habitudo autem creationis non sequitur motum, sed actionem divinam tantum, quae est prior quam creatura."

21. But one can imagine the question: is not likeness a function of mind that compares? But the datum that likeness is discovered by a mind does not render it purely a creation of mind: the objective hierarchy of act as limited in relation to potency is indeed a community not only in terms of relation to the first efficient and last final principle of the community— God, Who is known owing to the causal analysis in terms of the division of being by act and potency which defines the hierarchy of being—but also by virtue of the objective analogical similitude of act which is indeed the effect of God as *ipsum esse subsistens per se*, and which is known prior to and as a condition of attaining any natural knowledge of God. That there are logical and semantic aspects of the doctrine of analogy does not reduce the latter to the former.

22. It is because being is plurifiable only in relation to *potentia* that Thomas is able to argue that if there were a reality in which existence and essence were identical, then there could be only one, and then accordingly argue for the universality of the real distinction of essence and existence as applying even in the case of separate substances of which we have no quidditative knowledge. It is on the basis of this distinction universal to being (with but one possible exception) that he then immediately offers his existential proof for the existence of God. I say "proof" because it is a reasoned series of propositions ending in a deductive causal inference to the first cause. If this is not a proof, then the genus is empty. Below I cite the reference to the argumentation whereby Thomas indicates that since *a fortiori* if there were a being in which essence and existence were identical it could be subject to no potency, therefore if such a reality were to exist it would necessarily be unique. Such a reality could receive no further difference or form (because it would need to be in potency thereto), nor of matter (because it would be pure act, not material being). *De ente et essentia*, lib. 3: "Therefore it is clear that existence is distinct from essence or quiddity, unless perhaps there is a being whose quiddity is its very existence; and such a reality cannot be unless it be one and primary, because it is impossible that it be multiplied either by the addition of some difference, as the nature of the genus is multiplied in the species, or on account

of the reception of a form in diverse pieces of matter, as the nature of the species is multiplied in several individuals, or by reason of one of the things multiplied being separate and the other received in something; for example, if there were some separate warmth, then it would be separate from a non-separate warmth on account of its separation itself. However, if there were a thing that is existence only, so that it would be very subsistent existing itself, then this existence would not receive the addition of a difference, for then it would no longer be existence only, but existence and some form besides; and even less would it be receptive of the addition of matter, for then it would already be not subsistent, but material existence. Therefore, it remains that there can only be one thing that is its own existence." ("Ergo patet quod esse est aliud ab essentia vel quiditate, nisi forte sit aliqua res, cuius quiditas sit ipsum suum esse; et haec res non potest esse nisi una et prima, quia impossibile est, ut fiat plurificatio alicuius nisi per additionem alicuius differentiae, sicut multiplicatur natura generis in species, vel per hoc quod forma recipitur in diversis materiis, sicut multiplicatur natura speciei in diversis individuis, vel per hoc quod unum est absolutum et aliud in aliquo receptum, sicut si esset quidam calor separatus, esset alius a calore non separato ex ipsa sua separatione. Si autem ponatur aliqua res, quae sit esse tantum, ita ut ipsum esse sit subsistens, hoc esse non recipiet additionem differentiae, quia iam non esset esse tantum, sed esse et praeter hoc forma aliqua; et multo minus reciperet additionem materiae, quia iam esset esse non subsistens sed materiale. Unde relinquitur quod talis res, quae sit suum esse, non potest esse nisi una.")

23. *ST*, I, q. 44, art. 1, ad 3: "Now it is becoming that everything should have an efficient cause in proportion to its being." The finite being requires *actus purus* as its cause, because only pure act that is unreceived can account for the being of things whose act is limited and is received from without.

24. Ralph McInerny, *Aquinas and Analogy* (Washington, DC: Catholic University of America Press, 1996), 161–62.

25. *De veritate*, q. 2, art. 11, resp.

26. Without burdening Fr. Lawrence Dewan with an imputed responsibility for any of the ways in which my argument here may fall short, it seems to me with respect to the relation of metaphysics to logic that the observations in his essay "St. Thomas and Analogy: the Logician and the Metaphysician" are correct. Reprinted in his book *Form and Being: Studies in Thomistic Metaphysics* (Washington, DC: Catholic University of America Press, 2006). Indeed, even the logical principle of

noncontradiction is, I would argue, derivative of the metaphysical principle that being is not nonbeing, a principle which though it enumerates
no real plurality does articulate a real distinction rooted in being itself.
This is "real" in the same sense that it would be a truth founded in the real
nature of God that, even were there no existing creatures, "God is really
not a creature." There would be no real plurality—because no creatures—
but nonetheless a real distinction founded on the reality of the divine
nature. Likewise, something really is not nothing. The first principles
derived from our first knowledge of things are implicitly and actually
metaphysical principles from the start, on pain of never becoming so,
for what is not in the premises cannot make a suprise appearance in the
conclusion. Yet the concern to root metaphysics in the proper object of
the intellect—quiddity in corporeal matter—is also crucial, and I share
the concern for the immersion of our knowing in the intellective *contactus* with proportionate sensible being that seems to me to animate the
extraordinarily broad and penetrating work bequeathed to us through the
philosophic labors of Dr. McInerny.

27. McInerny's accomplishments in this regard, like those of Charles
De Konnick, are too profound, prolific, and well-known to require ennumeration here. Suffice it to be said that were one to think that these were
imperiled by the account of metaphysics put forward here, the present
author would happily abandon this account: but to the contrary, it seems
in no way necessary to the essential role of philosophy of nature that one
deny the knowability of proportionate being through abstraction by way
of the judgment of separation. Were it not for a certain fideizing of the
metaphysics of *esse* in certain quarters, and an equally unfortunate retreat
from the primacy of *natura* in theology and philosophy, the more common view of the Dominican commentatorial tradition on these matters
would perhaps have been more positively received.

28. Cf. the appendix on *separatio*, below.

29. See Thomas's *Commentary on Boethius's De trinitate*, q. 5, art. 1,
ad 6—the fuller text can be seen below, in the appendix, n. 6: "But we can
say that the science regarding potency or act or unity or other things of
this sort can be called part of metaphysics, because these are considered in
the same way as being, which is the subject of metaphysics." ("Sic autem
posset dici pars ipsius scientia, quae est de potentia vel quae est de actu
aut de uno vel de aliquo huiusmodi, quia ista habent eundem modum
considerandi cum ente, de quo tractatur in metaphysica.") Since the *per
se* is prior to the *per accidens*, the science of being as such, and of act and

potency as such, is presupposed by and implicit in the consideration of *ens in quantum mobile*, for it is matter that in order to be real needs to be, not being that absolutely requires matter.

30. Cf. Thomas's *Scriptum super Sententiis*, lib. 2, d. 1, q. 1, art. 5, ad 8; or simply the teaching of Thomas in *ST*, I, q. 13, art. 7 resp. and ad 4.

31. It is interesting that this exact point has come to the fore in the conversation put forward by profound minds of the *Communio* school of theology over the idea of finite being as a "subsistent relation"—an idea that falls short of seeing that the relations of the creature are consequent upon its creation, for a nonexistent thing has no relations, and a thing caused in its being is related rather than being a relation. Likewise when we speak of the creature's relation of participation to God, this is something real with respect to the creature (it is the relation of creature as effect to God as Cause) but it is not something real in God.

32. *ST*, I, q.13, art. 5, ad 1: "But this universal agent, although it is not univocal, still is not altogether equivocal, because then it could not produce its own likeness; but rather it is to be called an analogical agent, just as all univocal predications are reduced to one first non-univocal analogical predication, which is being." ("Hoc autem agens universale, licet non sit univocum, non tamen est omnino aequivocum, quia sic non faceret sibi simile; sed potest dici agens analogicum, sicut in praedicationibus omnia univoca reducuntur ad unum primum, non univocum, sed analogicum, quod est ens.")

33. *ST*, I, art. 3, art. 5, ad 1: "Therefore the universal cause of the whole species is not an univocal agent. But the universal cause comes before the particular cause. But this universal agent, while it is not univocal, still is not entirely equivocal, because otherwise it could not produce its own likeness; but it is able to be called an analogical agent, as all univocal predications are reduced to one first non-univocal analogical predication, which is being." ("Causa igitur universalis totius speciei non est agens univocum. Causa autem universalis est prior particulari. Hoc autem agens universale, licet non sit univocum, non tamen est omnino aequivocum, quia sic non faceret sibi simile; sed potest dici agens analogicum, sicut in praedicationibus omnia univoca reducuntur ad unum primum, non univocum, sed analogicum, quod est ens.")

34. *STAA*, 122.

35. This is the root of the claim that analogy of proper proportionality yields Maimonidean agnosticism with respect to divine perfections, whereas it does no such thing, but rather merely implies that there is no

determinate relation of God to creature, such that God is the fullness of all transcendental and pure perfections in such a way that the created mode wherein we grasp these is not applicable to God. Far from implying that God is perfect merely as cause of transcendental and pure perfections, this teaching asserts that God is Himself in His divine substance identified with the fullness of every transcendental or pure perfection freed from all created composition and limit of potency, and hence as immeasurably transcendent of finite participated perfection and as cause thereof. The divergence of this teaching from Maimonidean agnosis with respect to the divine perfections is pronounced.

36. It is indeed possible that many oppositions about Thomas's actual teaching are predicated on semantic confusion regarding terms, for what is a function of causal reasoning vis-à-vis the evidence of the analogy of being is put forward on some accounts as a "doctrine of analogy." But the evidentiary foundation of all such reasoning is the being of creatures, and that being is analogical by the analogy of proper proportionality before ever the existence of God is demonstrated. Further, the metaphysical proportioning of perfections either to created being as subject to the limits of potency, or to God as freed of all limit of potency, is a function of the analogy of being.

37. Of course, the proportion is that of identity of pure act to itself in God, whereas in the creature the proportion is the real ontological *ratio* of potency to act. The predicational analogy that Klubertanz cedes is certainly operative here. But the undergirding analogy of being which is the evidentiary foundation of metaphysical proof for God is that of proper proportionality, and with respect to finite being this analogy is clearly not merely predicative: being is, and can be, and can be said, in many ways, according to the likeness of diverse *rationes* of act and potency.

38. *STAA*, 122–23.

39. *STAA*, 123.

40. Of course, while the ontological proportions of potency and act constituting finite beings are real, there is in God only the proportion of pure act to itself, yet as supereminently containing every perfection without limit of potency.

41. God is really identical to Himself even though the relation of self-identity is a being of reason. *De potentia*, q. 7, art. 11, ad 3–5: "A man is really (and not merely conceptually) identical to himself, even though his relation [of self-identity] is a being of reason. And the explanation for this is that the cause of his relation is real—namely, the unity of his

substance, which our intellect considers under the aspect of a relation. In the same way, the power to compel subjects is really in God, and our intellect considers this power as ordered to the subjects because of the subjects' order to God. It is for this reason that he is really said to be Lord, even though his relation is a mere being of reason. And for the same reason it is evident that he would be Lord [Creator, etc.] even if there were no created intellect in existence." ("Ad tertium dicendum, quod sicut aliquis est idem sibi realiter, et non solum secundum rationem, licet relatio sit secundum rationem tantum, propter hoc quod relationis causa est realis, scilicet unitas substantiae quam intellectus sub relatione intelligit: ita potestas coercendi subditos est in Deo realiter, quam intellectus intelligit in ordine ad subditos propter ordinem subditorum ad ipsum; et propter hoc dicitur dominus realiter, licet relatio sit rationis tantum. Et eodem modo apparet quod dominus esset, nullo existente intellectu.")

42. *STAA*, 91.

43. *STAA*, 92: "It is noteworthy that in its Aristotelian source and in at least one other Thomistic usage (see above, page 80) this example appears under the rubric of proportionality and seems much more reasonably to be a proportionality." But is it likely that when Thomas uses the language of proportionality earlier, that he did not mean it or understand it to signify in this way but viewed it to be essentially quantitative? This seems, to this author, extremely unlikely. The quantitative example is a didactic aid in moving the student to understand by contrast genuine analogy of proper proportionality, which does not consist in any univocal quantitative object.

44. *STAA*, 121–22.

45. John F. Wippel, *The Metaphysical Thought of Thomas Aquinas* (Washington, DC: Catholic University of America Press, 2000), 554.

46. *De potentia dei*, q. 7, art.10, ad 9: "Ad nonum dicendum, quod si proportio intelligatur aliquis determinatus excessus, nulla est Dei ad creaturam proportio. Si autem per proportionem intelligatur habitudo sola, sic patet quod est inter creatorem et creaturam; in creatura quidem realiter, non autem in creatore."

47. *The Sources of Catholic Dogma*, trans. Roy J. Deferrario (St. Louis and London: Herder, 1957.) [Original: Heinrich Denzinger, *Enchiridion Symbolorum*, 30th ed. (Freiburg: Herder, 1954)], #432, p. 171, the Constitutions of the Fourth Lateran Council, under point 2, "On the Error of Abbot Joachim." For the full text see ch. 2, n. 6, above.

Chapter Four. The Analogy of Being and the Transcendence
and Analogical Intelligibility of the Act of Faith

1. This, it would seem, is the world J.-L. Marion is left with in a 1995 essay, which while clearing Thomas of the charges that Marion had earlier placed against him moves one no further toward understanding any rational basis for discourse about God. "Saint Thomas d'Aquin et l'onto-théo-logie," *Revue Thomiste* 95, no. 1 (1995): 31–66. But then Marion, like most moderns, has learned to discount the metaphysics and natural philosophy of Thomas, insisting upon superordinating Enlightenment and post-Enlightenment categories to an account built on wholly other—and wholly defensible—premises.

2. Of course, the earlier observations regarding participation are pertinent here. See ch. 1, nn. 13–18, above.

3. Jacques Maritain, *The Degrees of Knowledge*, 4th ed., trans. Gerald B. Phelan, presented by Ralph McInerny (Notre Dame, IN: University of Notre Dame Press, 1995), 256–57.

4. *ST*, I, q. 13, art. 1, resp.: "Ostensum est autem supra quod Deus in hac vita non potest a nobis videri per suam essentiam; sed cognoscitur a nobis ex creaturis, secundum habitudinem principii, et per modum excellentiae et remotionis. Sic igitur potest nominari a nobis ex creaturis, non tamen ita quod nomen significans ipsum . . ."

Appendix. A (Very) Few Words Regarding
Metaphysics, Separatio, *and* Abstractio

1. Here one sees how the improper causal analogy enriches our understanding, in that we see that the whole of the created effects constitutes a work of divine art. Yet this very insight requires, proceeds from, and as it were "converts back into" the *analogia entis* in terms of proper proportionality, for the divine artist infinitely exceeds all His effects.

2. This is, of course, not least of importance to programs of Catholic studies which seek to give students a broad exposure to the elements of Catholic theology and culture.

3. Cf. St. Thomas Aquinas, *Commentary on Boethius's De trinitate* (hereinafter cited as *CBDT*), q. 5, art. 3, resp.

4. For this whole discussion, of course, see *CBDT*, q. 5, art. 3, resp.

5. Cf. Fr. John Wippel's famed essay, "Metaphysics and *Separa-tio* according to St. Thomas Aquinas," *Review of Metaphysics* 31 (1978): 431–70; it is reprinted in his *Metaphysical Themes in St. Thomas Aquinas* (Washington, DC: Catholic University of America Press, 1984), 69–104.

6. *CBDT*, q. 5, art. 1, ad 6: "Albeit subjects of the other sciences are parts of being, which is the subject of metaphysics, still the other sciences are not necessarily parts of metaphysics. For each science considers one part of being in a special way distinct from the way in which metaphysics treats of being. Wherefore properly speaking its subject is not part of the subject of metaphysics, for it is not part of being according to the intelligible measure whereby being is the subject of metaphysics, but considered in this way is a special science distinguished from the others. But we can say that the science regarding potency or act or unity or other things of this sort can be called part of metaphysics, because these are considered in the same way as being, which is the subject of metaphysics." Note in particular the comment regarding "the science regarding potency"— a suggestive observation with respect to the consideration of *potentia* in sensible being, showing how certain critical judgments in the philosophy of nature are implicitly and actually metaphysical. ("Ad sextum dicendum quod quamvis subiecta aliarum scientiarum sint partes entis, quod est subiectum metaphysicae, non tamen oportet quod aliae scientiae sint partes ipsius. Accipit enim unaquaeque scientiarum unam partem entis secundum specialem modum considerandi alium a modo, quo consideratur ens in metaphysica. Unde proprie loquendo subiectum illius non est pars subiecti metaphysicae; non enim est pars entis secundum illam rationem, qua ens est subiectum metaphysicae, sed hac ratione considerata ipsa est specialis scientia aliis condivisa. Sic autem posset dici pars ipsius scientia, quae est de potentia vel quae est de actu aut de uno vel de aliquo huiusmodi, quia ista habent eundem modum considerandi cum ente, de quo tractatur in metaphysica.")

7. *ST*, I, q. 85, art. 1, ad 1: "Ad primum ergo dicendum quod abstrahere contingit dupliciter. Uno modo, per modum compositionis et divisionis; sicut cum intelligimus aliquid non esse in alio, vel esse separatum ab eo. Alio modo, per modum simplicis et absolutae considerationis; sicut cum intelligimus unum, nihil considerando de alio. Abstrahere igitur per intellectum ea quae secundum rem non sunt abstracta, secundum primum modum abstrahendi, non est absque falsitate. Sed secundo modo abstrahere per intellectum quae non sunt abstracta secundum rem, non habet falsitatem; ut in sensibilibus manifeste apparet."

8. *ST,* I, q. 85, art. 1, ad 2: "Possunt tamen considerari sine hac vel illa substantia; quod est eas abstrahi a materia intelligibili individuali. Quaedam vero sunt quae possunt abstrahi etiam a materia intelligibili communi, sicut ens, unum, potentia et actus, et alia huiusmodi, quae etiam esse possunt absque omni materia, ut patet in substantiis immaterialibus. Et quia Plato non consideravit quod dictum est de duplici modo abstractionis, omnia quae diximus abstrahi per intellectum, posuit abstracta esse secundum rem."

9. Cf. *CBDT,* q. 5, art. 4, wherein St. Thomas teaches that philosophers consider God only as principle of all things, in relation to being *qua* being: not as the subject of the science (for that is being) but as the principle of the subject. This is in contrast to revealed theology, which considers God as the very subject of the science.

10. *CBDT,* q. 5, art. 4, resp.: "There is another theology which considers divine things for their own sakes as the subject of the science and it is this theology that is entrusted and communicated in sacred scripture." ("Alia vero, quae ipsas res divinas considerat propter se ipsas ut subiectum scientiae et haec est theologia, quae in sacra Scriptura traditur.")

11. *CBDT,* q. 5, art. 4, resp.: "Utraque autem est de his quae sunt separata a materia et motu secundum esse, sed diversimode, secundum quod dupliciter potest esse aliquid a materia et motu separatum secundum esse. Uno modo sic, quod de ratione ipsius rei, quae separata dicitur, sit quod nullo modo in materia et motu esse possit, sicut Deus et Angeli dicuntur a materia et motu separati. Alio modo sic, quod non sit de ratione eius quod sit in materia et motu, sed possit esse sine materia et motu, quamvis quandoque inveniatur in materia et motu. Et sic ens et substantia et potentia et actus sunt separata a materia et motu, quia secundum esse a materia et motu non dependent, sicut mathematica dependebant, quae numquam nisi in materia esse possunt, quamvis sine materia sensibili possint intelligi. Theologia ergo philosophica determinat de separatis secundo modo sicut de subiectis, de separatis autem primo modo sicut de principiis subiecti."

12. Aquinas, *prooemium* to the *Commentary on the Metaphysics*: "Quia secundum esse et rationem separari dicuntur, non solum illa quae nunquam in materia esse possunt, sicut Deus et intellectuales substantiae, sed etiam illa quae possunt sine materia esse, sicut ens commune. Hoc tamen non contingeret, si a materia secundum esse dependerent."

13. *CBDT,* q. 5, art. 4, ad 5: "Ad quintum dicendum quod ens et substantia dicuntur separata a materia et motu non per hoc quod de ratione

ipsorum sit esse sine materia et motu, sicut de ratione asini est sine ratione esse, sed per hoc quod de ratione eorum non est esse in materia et motu, quamvis quandoque sint in materia et motu, sicut animal abstrahit a ratione, quamvis aliquod animal sit rationale."

14. *Existence and the Existent*, 28 n. 14.

15. *Existence and the Existent*, 30, part of the extensive n. 14 that begins on p. 28.

16. *Existence and the Existent*, 30 n. 14.

17. Cf. *ST*, I, q. 7, art. 1, resp.: "Illud autem quod est maxime formale omnium, est ipsum esse . . ."

18. It is often thought that Maritain's notion of an intuition of being was a Bergsonian superimposition upon the teaching of Thomas. But however many respects there are in which his account may have Bergsonian aspects, insofar as he means by this language to refer to the intellectual judgment that what is most formal in being is act; that act is not self-limiting; and that this is manifest in the truth that being overpasses and is irreducible to any of its contractive modes such that being is intrinsically analogous; just so far does his account seem to be a reasoned and true understanding of the teaching of Aquinas.

Index

Steven A. Long

is professor of theology

at Ave Maria University in Naples, Florida.